A WEE GUIDE TO

The Jacobites

WITH **50** GREAT JACOBITE SITES TO VISIT
AND ICONIC *OUTLANDER* LOCATIONS

Charles Sinclair

GOBLINSHEAD
COCKENZIE HOUSE

First Published 1998
Reprinted 2001, reset with updating 2008, updated 2015,
updated 2018 with *Outlander* locations
© Martin Coventry 1998, 2008, 2015, 2018

GOBLINSHEAD

Cockenzie House, 22 Edinburgh Road,
Cockenzie, East Lothian EH32 0HY
www.goblinshead.co.uk
www.thecastlesofscotland.co.uk / www.castlesoftheclans.co.uk
www.bogles.co.uk

British Library Cataloguing in Publication Data
A catalogue record for this book is available from the British Library.

ISBN 978 1899874 14 9

Printed by Bell and Bain, Glasgow, Scotland

www.thecastlesofscotland.co.uk/the-best-castles/outlander/

See **www.goblinshead.co.uk** for new, forthcoming and popular
Scottish titles, articles on Scottish history and famous Scots,, places to
visit with websites, ghosts and witches, and much more…

WEE GUIDES
Scottish History
Prehistoric Scotland • The Picts
• St Margaret and Malcolm Canmore
William Wallace • Robert the Bruce
Mary, Queen of Scots
Rob Roy MacGregor • The Jacobites • Flora MacDonald
Robert Burns • Whisky
Scottish Ghosts and Bogles

Contents

List of Maps

List of Illustrations

Acknowledgements

Thanks to everyone who made this wee book possible, particularly Martin Coventry who had sufficient faith to let an opinionated old so and so write a book about his favourite area. I must also mention Joyce Miller, for all her hard work, and Isla Robertson, at the Picture Library of the NTS, for being so understanding.

Thanks to the Scottish National Portrait Gallery for the following illustrations: Prince Henry Benedict, formerly thought to be Charles Edward Stewart by Maurice Quentin de la Tour (front cover); James, Duke of York, (James VII and II) by Sir Peter Lely (page 14); James VIII and III by François de Troy (1701) (page 19); John Graham of Claverhouse, Viscount Dundee, by unknown artist (page 21); John Erskine, Earl of Mar, from the studio of Sir Geoffrey Kneller (page 39); Bonnie Prince Charlie by Antonio David (page 46); Lord George Murray by Sir Robert Strange (page 51); Bonnie Prince Charlie attributed to Hugh Douglas Hamilton (page 68). Thanks to the United Service War Museum for the permission to use the Death of Colonel Gardner (at the Battle of Prestonpans), from an engraving by R. C. Bell after Sir William Allan (page 53). Many thanks also to The National Trust of Scotland for the following illustrations: Killiecrankie (page 22); Glencoe (page 25); Glenfinnan (page 49); Culloden memorial (page 61); Culloden memorial (page 74); Glenfinnan memorial (page 79) and Killiecrankie (page 82). Maps and other photos and illustrations by Martin Coventry.

How to Use this Book

This book is divided into two sections:

- The text (pages 2-69) describes the times of the Jacobites and the events surrounding them, covering the events leading up to the 'abdication' of James VII and III, the Jacobite Rising of 1689 led by Bonnie Dundee, the 1715 by 'Bobbing John' Earl of Mar, and the '45 by Bonnie Prince Charlie. There are 5 maps (pages 4, 36, 48, 50 & 55), and a family tree illustrates the relationship of the Stewart and Hanoverian monarchs (page 32). A calendar of events summarises the period chronologically (page 2-3).

- Places to visit associated with the Jacobites (pages 70-85) listing more than 50 sites, including Culloden battlefield (page 74). Information includes access, opening, facilities, and a brief description; and a map locates all the sites in Scotland (page 70). Further sites are given in list form at the end of the section (page 84-5).

Outlander locations are listed with visitor information (page 86-90).
www.thecastlesofscotland.co.uk/the-best-castles/outlander/

Disclaimer:

The information contained in this Wee Guide to the Jacobites (the "Material") is believed to be accurate at the time of printing, but no representation or warranty is given (express or implied) as to its accuracy, completeness or correctness. The author and publisher do not accept any liability whatsoever for any direct, indirect or consequential loss or damage arising in any way from any use of or reliance on this Material for any purpose.

While every care has been taken to compile and check all the information in this book, in a work of this complexity it is possible that mistakes and omissions may have occurred. If you know of any corrections, alterations or improvements, please contact the publishers.

Introduction

The Jacobites remain misted in romanticism and nostalgia: the Scottish kings deposed by the English, the last ditch attempt of the Highlands – and indeed Scotland itself – to remain free of southern domination. Bonnie Prince Charlie, handsome and brave, still inspires a song and a tear in these later days. Many have listed the tragic battle of Culloden as a fight between the Sassenach and the Scot, between the butchering English and noble Highlander.

The story of the Jacobites is a fascinating one, but is not as simple as much of the mythology. James VII – whose supporters were first called Jacobites after he had fled to France – was as unpopular in Scotland as in England. The Jacobites were more interested in regaining the English throne than the Scottish. More Scots fought in the Hanoverian army under Butcher Cumberland than fought for the Jacobites.

One event certainly is clear: the tragedy of the Battle of Culloden, where wounded Jacobites were bayoneted, shot or clubbed to death, and the whole Highland way of life was subsequently obliterated.

This small book relates the fascinating but ultimately tragic events surrounding the Jacobites, and describes many of the devious, noble, proud, brave and unlucky players in their tale.

I hope you find their story as engrossing as I have.

CS, Musselburgh, March 1998

We have taken the opportunity of this printing to completely update the visitor information in the places to visit section, along with adding postcodes.

CS, Musselburgh, August 2015

As well as completely updating the visitor information in the places to visit section, we have also added a section on *Outlander* locations from the popular TV series, with visitor information and access. Goblinshead is now located at Cockenzie House, from where the baggage train with many valuables was seized in 1745 by Jacobites after victory at the nearby Battle of Prestonpans.

CS, Cockenzie, July 2018

Calendar of Events

1633	James, Duke of York – later James VII of Scots and II of England – born.
1636-7	Charles I tries to reintroduce Episcopal church in Scotland.
1638	National Covenant signed by Charles I's opponents.
1642-6	Civil War; Charles I eventually defeated; Cromwell governs England.
1649	Charles I executed. Scots rise against Cromwell.
1650-60	Scots defeated by Cromwell; English invade Scotland and impose Commonwealth.
1660	Restoration of Charles II. James, Duke of York, marries Anne Hyde. They have two daughters: Mary and Anne.
1666	Pentland rising; Covenanters defeated at Rullion Green.
1668	James converts to Roman Catholicism.
1673	James marries Mary of Modena after death of Anne Hyde.
1679	Unrest in Scotland; Battle of Drumclog; Battle of Bothwell Brig; Covenanters defeated.
1681-5	'Killing Times'; further persecution of Covenanters.
1685	Charles II dies. Succession of James VII of Scots and II of England. Monmouth's Rising, supported in Scotland by Earl of Argyll. Rising fails and both executed.
1688	Birth of James Francis Edward 'the Old Pretender'. Revolution against James VII and II; James flees to France.
1689	William of Orange and Mary proclaimed joint monarchs; Jacobites, supporters of James VII, led by Claverhouse; Battle of Killiecrankie; Jacobites victorious but Claverhouse killed; Jacobites disband after defeat at Dunkeld.
1690	Jacobites defeated at Cromdale; and at Battle of Boyne in Ireland; Presbyterian church reintroduced in Scotland.
1692	Massacre of Glencoe.
1694	Mary, wife of William of Orange, dies.
1695-1700	Company of Scotland formed; disaster of Darien Scheme.
1701	Death of James VII and II; Act of Settlement: Crown to go to Hanover; James Francis Edward 'the Old Pretender' recognised as king by France and Spain.
1702	William of Orange dies, succeeded by Anne.
1703	Act Anent Peace and War (Scotland).

1704	Act of Security (Scotland).
1705	Alien Act (England) forces Scotland to treat for Union of Parliaments. Commissioners appointed to negotiate Union.
1706	Scottish parliament pass first of Articles of Treaty of Union.
1707	Scottish parliament dissolved; parliament of Great Britain established.
1708	Aborted campaign by James VIII to return to Scotland.
1714	Anne dies, succession of the Hanoverian George I.
1715	Standard raised for James VIII and III at Braemar by Earl of Mar; Battle of Sheriffmuir; Jacobites defeated at Battle of Preston; James VIII lands at Peterhead.
1716	Jacobites disband; James VIII returns to France.
1719	Spanish-backed campaign; Jacobites seize Eilean Donan Castle; Battle of Glen Shiel; Jacobites defeated. James VIII marries Clementina Sobieski.
1720	Birth of Bonnie Prince Charlie: Charles Edward 'the Young Pretender'.
1724-44	Roads built in north of Scotland by General Wade.
1727	George I dies; succeeded by George II.
1745	Charles Edward 'the Young Pretender' raises Jacobite Standard at Glenfinnan; Jacobites capture Edinburgh; victory at Battle of Prestonpans; Jacobites advance into England; reach Derby, but then decide to retreat north.
1746	Charles Edward meets Clementina Walkinshaw, who becomes his mistress. Jacobite victory at Battle of Falkirk; Battle of Culloden: Jacobites crushed by 'Butcher' Cumberland. Charles a fugitive in the Highlands for several months; rescued by French ship; returns to Continent, but never returns to Scotland; severe retribution against Jacobites and Highlanders.
1747	Clementina Walkinshaw gives birth to Charles's daughter, Charlotte.
1772	Charles marries Princess Louise of Stolberg. They have no children and she eventually leaves him.
1788	Charles dies in Rome without legitimate child.
1807	Henry Benedict, Cardinal York, Charles's brother dies. End of the Jacobite cause.

Map 1: Scotland 1633-1707

1–James, Duke of York

The Jacobites in general, and Bonnie Prince Charlie in particular, have become romance incarnate, the very thing of Scottish myth and legend, the King over the sea, the Old Pretender, the Young Chevalier – 'Will ye no come back again?' Yet the truth is much less obscured by Scotch mist.

The Jacobite cause was born in 1689 when James VII of Scots and II of England removed himself and his family from England after the arrival of a force led by William of Orange. William was married to Mary, James's daughter, and was a staunch Protestant. James VII was a Roman Catholic, and when his son, James Francis Edward 'the Old Pretender' was born, both Scotland and England rebelled against his rule, dismayed by the possibility of a new Roman Catholic dynasty. William of Orange, who was also James's nephew, and Mary were invited to become joint monarchs. James fled to France, and John Graham of Claverhouse, Viscount Dundee, raised an army for James – the Latin form of which is *Jacob*, hence Jacobites – and so began the Jacobite Risings.

These were not, however, conflicts primarily between the English and the Scots, nor even between the Highlands and the Lowlands. It is true that many in Scotland were unhappy with William's rule, and the monarchs that followed, but just as many were reluctant to see the Stewarts restored, not least many Protestants, Covenanters and Cameronians. There proved to be little support for the Jacobites in England and Wales, although some Scots had a residual loyalty to the Scottish Stewarts. Many Lowlanders and Highlanders, however, supported both William and the Hanoverian kings, including the Campbells, Semples, Cathcarts, Munros, MacKays and Grants. Others remained neutral, or changed sides as events, chance or fortune suited.

The Massacre of Glencoe in 1692, the disaster of the Darien Scheme in the late 1690s, and then English arrogance after the Union of Parliaments in 1707 did increase resentment in Scotland, and the Jacobites provided a focus for this anger. James VII, and then his son: James Francis Edward – James VIII and III 'the Old Pretender' – and grandson: Charles Edward Stewart – Bonnie Prince Charlie 'the

Young Pretender' – kept the Jacobite cause alive. But increasingly it was European powers, regularly at war with Britain, who instigated and supported the Risings, and the Jacobites became pawns in wider European politics.

The Rising of 1745-46 seemed the least likely to succeed, but the charm and charisma of its leader, Charles Edward Stewart – Bonnie Prince Charlie – raised an army made up mostly of Highlanders and troops from the north. Initially the Rising went well, with the decisive victory at the Battle of Prestonpans, the advance to Derby in England, and promised support from the French and Spanish. But then came retreat, and the disaster of the Battle of Culloden on 16 April 1746: the Rising and the Jacobite cause ended in a red mist of grapeshot, musket fire and bayonets; but the Hanoverian retribution did not

Drumossie Moor, Culloden, scene of the battle in 1746 when the Jacobites were defeated.

end here. What followed the battle was the planned, and brutally executed, destruction of the whole of the Highland way of life, which finally culminated in the Clearances and depopulation of the Highlands.

Perhaps it is better to think that the Jacobite cause and Bonnie Prince Charlie were worth the sacrifice, but the truth is that Charles

Edward Stewart – often called *Stuart* from a French misspelling of the name in the time of Mary, Queen of Scots – died in Rome, debauched and drunken, deserted by nearly all his supporters except his illegitimate daughter and Cardinal brother.

'Will you no come back again?' goes the song. Well, he never did, and Scotland may not have been worse for it.

To understand the Jacobites, however, it is necessary to go back to the reign of Charles's great-grandfather, Charles I, and look at the events surrounding him and his son James, later James VII of Scots and II of England.

James was born in October 1633. He was the son of Charles I and Henrietta Maria, daughter of Henry IV of France, and was given the title Duke of York shortly after his birth. He had an older brother, Charles, later Charles II. This was a time of religious turmoil and strife – a state of affairs which had continued since the Reformation in the 1560s.

In Scotland Protestantism had taken firm hold, and there had been efforts to establish Presbyterianism from 1592: a more democratic system of church organisation, where representatives were elected by their peers. The church was organised into kirk sessions, presbyteries, synods, and a General Assembly. The Protestants believed that there were two kingdoms: the secular one, controlled by the monarch; and the religious one, controlled by God, who ultimately had overall supremacy, even over the king. James's father, Charles I, made himself unpopular, both in Scotland and England, by his high-handed desire to rule absolutely. This included trying to impose a unified Episcopal church – controlled by bishops, appointed by the monarch – in both countries, firmly under his control. Charles believed himself to be the supreme head of the Church.

With no general support from either the Scottish or English parliament or the agreement of a General Assembly, Charles I firstly forced the *Code of Canons* – which emphasised royal supremacy, and ignored kirk sessions, presbyteries and the General Assembly; then a revised liturgy *The Book of Common Prayer* on the Scots in 1636-7. Although much in the Prayer Book was acceptable to the

Protestants, parts of the liturgy dealing with the communion were controversial, other parts were open to interpretation, which the monarch could change as desired according to royal supremacy.

There were widespread protests, and a riot in St Giles Cathedral in Edinburgh, when Jenny Geddes – possibly a mythical Scottish figure – is said to have thrown her stool at the minister.

This and other measures, such as the imposition of a direct tax system and the 1625 Act of Revocation, according to which all grants of church and royal property were to be restored to the Crown, led to much discontent among both the nobility and general populace. This culminated in the signing of the National Covenant in 1638, asserting the rights of the people over the monarch.

Conflict smouldered on for several years, but at last flared into civil warfare in 1642.

After a long conflict and many battles – called wrongly the 'English' Civil War as it did, in fact, affect all of the British Isles, including Ireland – by 1646 Charles and the Royalist side had been defeated by the Parliamentarians under Cromwell, with Scottish help. Charles was captured by the Scots, but was turned over to the English and imprisoned. Without consulting the Scots, however, the King was executed in 1649 by order of an unrepresentative English parliament.

Dunnottar Castle – see next page.

Charles II, elder brother of James, was proclaimed king in Scotland. The Scots, angered by the execution of his father, rose against Cromwell; but the resistance was badly managed and Cromwell defeated the Scots at the Battle of Dunbar in 1650, the last stronghold Dunnottar had fallen by 1652, and Scotland was occupied from Shetland to Stranraer.

James, Duke of York, had been a spectator at the indecisive Battle of Edgehill in 1642, and was then taken to the Royalist headquarters at Oxford, where he stayed for the remainder of the war. He was made a prisoner of Parliament in 1646, but fled abroad in 1648, after escaping from London disguised as a girl. James earned a reputation for courage when he served as a soldier in France, earning the rank of Lieutenant General. He also fought in Spain in 1658, where he was made an Admiral.

In 1660, after the death of Cromwell and the collapse of his Commonwealth, Charles II was invited to return to Britain and become King of England, Wales and Scotland. Charles II and James, Duke of York, his brother, returned to England, and the new king appointed John Maitland, 1st Duke of Lauderdale, as Secretary of State for Scotland: Charles never visited Scotland after 1660, and Lauderdale virtually ruled the country for the next 20 years. Corruption and injustice were rife.

Episcopacy was restored in Scotland, although Charles II had actually signed the National Covenant in 1651, a document used to condemn the episcopal system. Conventicles – meetings of Covenanters to worship and preach – were outlawed. James Sharp was made Archbishop of St Andrews in 1661, and under Sharp and Lauderdale, although there were periods of greater tolerance, religious strife continued. This led to the Pentland Rising of Covenanters in 1666, which was crushed at the Battle of Rullion Green by government dragoons under General Tam Dalziel. Thirty prisoners were hanged, while others were transported to Barbados. In October 1667, however, an amnesty was announced for those who would swear not to bear arms against the king.

2–The Killing Times

Unrest continued and conventicles spread. The 'Highland Host' – troops made up of thousands of Highland and Lowland militia – were quartered by Lauderdale on disaffected Covenanters in Ayrshire and the west, in an attempt to force them into line. The policy was hugely unpopular, and the Highlanders pillaged the area, increasing sympathy for the Covenanters and leaving a lasting fear and hatred of Highlanders.

Then in 1679, while crossing Magus Moor near St Andrews, Archbishop Sharp was cruelly murdered by Covenanters. Sharp was dragged from his carriage and, in front of his daughter, was shot, slashed, trampled and had his skull crushed.

James, Duke of York, meanwhile, had been made High Lord Admiral of England by Charles II, a post which he held from 1660 to 1673. He greatly improved the navy during this period, which he may have later regretted. In 1660 he married Anne Hyde, a daughter of the Earl of Clarendon. She had become his mistress while they were in exile. The couple were married a month before their first child was born, and they had two daughters, Mary and Anne, who would later both be monarchs in their own right.

In 1664 Charles bestowed on James the American provinces previously controlled by the Dutch, and the name was changed to New York in his honour. James converted to Roman Catholicism in 1668, as had Anne Hyde, and two years later he was a party to the secret Treaty of Dover in which Charles II admitted his own conversion, and decided to restore the kingdom to Roman Catholicism. Anne Hyde died in 1671; and in 1673, James married Mary of Modena, who was a devout Roman Catholic. Parliament then tried to pass the Exclusion Bill, an attempt to bar accession to the throne by a Roman Catholic. James was sent north in 1679 to govern Scotland, largely because his presence in London was helping the backers of the Bill.

The situation in Scotland, meanwhile, continued to worsen, and this came to battle on 1 June 1679 at Drumclog, near Strathaven. John Graham of Claverhouse – later to take a major part in the first of the

Jacobite Risings – and a force of government dragoons were humiliatingly defeated by a heavily armed party of Covenanters, who were holding an illegal conventicle. The Covenanters were heartened by the victory, support grew, and they quickly raised an army, although they slew the small number of prisoners they had taken after the battle.

John Graham of Claverhouse, son of a Royalist family, had fought in France for Louis XIV, under the Duke of Monmouth and MacKay of Scourie. He is said to have saved the life of William of Orange at the Battle of Seneff. Claverhouse escaped from the fighting at Drumclog, helped defend Glasgow, then joined the Duke of Monmouth.

The Covenanters' victory was short lived, and they were soon riven by dissent. At the Battle of Bothwell Brig on 22 June 1679, they were crushed by government troops led by James Duke of Monmouth (and Buccleuch) and Claverhouse. The Covenanters fought bravely, led by David Hackston of Rathillet, but to no avail, and many were executed, while 1200 others were imprisoned in Greyfriars' Kirkyard in Edinburgh before being transported.

Although Drumclog was a minor battle, Lauderdale, as Secretary of State and King's Commissioner from 1669, was blamed; and in 1680

Greyfriar's Kirkyard – it was here that the National Covenant was first signed in 1638, but the Kirkyard was used to imprison Covenanters after the Battle of Bothwell Brig in 1679.

replaced by the James Duke of Monmouth, Charles II's illegitimate son. Monmouth's administration was more tolerant, and many prisoners were released.

James, Duke of York, then replaced Monmouth, but under his rule, and then under that of James Drummond, Earl of Perth, the persecution of Covenanters greatly increased. Claverhouse – with others such as Sir George 'Bloody' Mackenzie of Rosehaugh, the Lord Advocate; Sir Robert Grierson of Lagg; and the 'Bloody' Bruce of Earlshall – were bloodily blamed for many atrocities. Claverhouse, known as 'Bloody Clavers', presided at the execution of the Wigtown Martyrs: two women who were bound to posts to be drowned by the incoming tide – although there is some doubt as to whether they actually drowned.

Men were more quickly dealt with, just being shot. These were the 'Killing Times', and although acts of cruelty were numerous, probably only around 100 people were summarily killed. Claverhouse is said to have been responsible for the deaths of ten Covenanters.

Some of the most determined and fanatical Covenanters continued to resist, but although many Scots had sympathy for them, few supported their ex-

Memorial to the Wigtown Martyrs.

treme aims. Led by Richard Cameron, Donald Cargill and Hackston of Rathillet, they became known as the Cameronians or 'Society People'.

On 22 June 1680, Cameron made a Declaration at Sanquhar, repudiating Charles II and disowning him as King, as well as declaring war on him and his followers. His small band of Cameronians was waylaid by government forces at Airds Moss shortly afterwards. Cameron was slain, his head and hands being hacked off and taken to Edinburgh, where they were displayed at the Netherbow. Cargill then excommunicated Charles II, James, Monmouth and other leaders, but was captured in May 1681 and beheaded at Edinburgh's Mercat Cross. Hackston was hanged, after his hands had been cut off.

But dissent continued, and further measures were taken against the Covenanters. The Test Act of 1681 ordered that every holder of public office should take an oath upholding the 1560 Confession of Faith, which among other things confirmed royal supremacy over the Church; and demanded renunciation of the Covenant. Eight of the Episcopal clergy resigned, as well as 60 others; so did Sir James Dalrymple, President of the Court of Session; and Archibald Campbell, 9th Earl of Argyll, who had to flee abroad, disguised as a page, after being sentenced to death. James, himself, was exempted from the oath, as it would have barred him from office.

In November 1684 the Apologetical Declaration was posted on several market-crosses and churches. Composed by James Renwick, now the leader of the Cameronians, it warned anyone who tried to capture or kill them would do so at the risk of their own lives. This gave Claverhouse and Mackenzie an excuse for further harshness and persecution. Covenanter prisoners were asked to denounce the Declaration, but if they did not they were shot.

Charles II died of a stroke on 6 February 1685. Since the Restoration of 1660, he had not visited Scotland. His two aims, however, had been achieved: he had maintained his position as monarch of both England and Scotland; and had strengthened the Crown and made the monarchy well-nigh absolute. He had also secured the succession of his brother, although James was openly a Roman Catholic.

3–James VII of Scots and II of England

James was proclaimed King of Scots on 10 February 1685 at the age of 51; and although he promised 'to defend and support' the Episcopalian Church of England – he declined to take the Coronation Oath to defend the Protestant religion. Parliament voted him the most generous funding ever bestowed on a Stewart monarch. When Parliament met in April, however, a new Act once more declared the taking of the Covenants to be treason, and made the mere attendance at a conventicle punishable by death.

James VII and II, when Duke of York, by Sir Peter Lely (SNPG).

James seemed to be in a very strong position, highlighted by the failure of Monmouth's rising, supported in Scotland by Archibald Campbell, 9th Earl of Argyll. In June 1685 Argyll landed in Kintyre with 300 men. The rebellion had little support, and Argyll was captured – although he had tried to commit suicide by shooting himself – and then beheaded in Edinburgh. His supporters and sympathisers were harshly treated, and his lands were ravaged by rival clans. To help persuade others not to rebel in Scotland, 167

Covenanters were imprisoned in a vault at Dunnottar Castle during a hot summer, where many died, while others were transported. Monmouth fared little better when he invaded the south of England. His forces were defeated at the Battle of Sedgemoor on 6 July, and nine days later he was beheaded on Tower Hill in London.

Increased persecution of Protestants in France led to a riot against Roman Catholic priests in Edinburgh. James, nevertheless, appointed Roman Catholics to the offices of Chancellor and Secretary of State, and at the Parliament of 1686 recommended the repeal of the penal laws against innocent Roman Catholics. When the Scottish Parliament refused, James ordered the Privy Council to annul the laws. Letters of Indulgence, issued in 1687, allowed Roman Catholics and Protestants to serve God in their own way, provided they did not encourage disloyalty to the Crown. As a result James earned the gratitude of the Quakers, as this gave them freedom from persecution – but little else.

The Indulgence, however, did not extend to conventicles, and it did not pardon the Cameronians. The last of their ministers, James Renwick, was captured and executed in 1688. The Indulgence did allow Presbyterian ministers to return to their parishes, where their influence played a large part in what was to follow.

In April 1688, seven bishops refused to read James's Declaration of Indulgence from their pulpits, and were brought to trial; although they were acquitted. Their arrest stirred resentment, already simmering because of the promotion of Roman Catholics to positions of power.

The final straw, however, was on 10 June when Mary of Modena, James's wife, gave birth to a son James Francis Edward – 'the Old Pretender'.

This convinced many in both Scotland and England that James's policies would succeed him after his death, that a new Roman Catholic dynasty would be founded.

The child's parentage was questioned: the somewhat far-fetched and oft-used claim being that the pregnancy had been faked, that the child had been brought to Mary in a warming pan. Meanwhile, William of Orange, James's nephew and a staunch Protestant, landed on 5 November at Torbay on the south coast of England. His army included many disaffected Scots.

James lost his nerve and panicked, taken unawares by this turn of events, and eventually fled to France on 23 December. It was claimed by the English that he abdicated by fleeing, so leaving the throne vacant for William and Mary. William accepted the English throne on 13 February 1689.

William of Orange had married Mary – his own cousin and daughter of James VII by Anne Hyde – in 1677 when she was 15. He was 12 years older. The couple do not appear to have been close: Mary is said to have wept for more than a day when she was told that the marriage had been arranged; and they had no children. William, however, had left Mary behind when he arrived in England, demanding that he be made joint sovereign with her or he would return to Holland. He, in turn, agreed that questions of Church and State should be settled by a free Parliament, and the English proclaimed him king.

Scottish Episcopalians had no wish to be ruled by William, a Dutch Protestant, and many others, both in Scotland and England, remained loyal to James; but the Scots were surprised and divided by James's flight. The Scottish Chancellor John Drummond, Earl of Perth, was driven from his house in Edinburgh, because he was a Roman Catholic; and the Roman Catholic Chapel at Holyrood was sacked and

Holyrood – the church was ransacked by a mob in 1688.

despoiled. On Christmas day some 200 Episcopalian ministers were turned out of their homes in the south west.

William summoned a meeting of the Scottish Estates in Edinburgh on 14 March 1689, agreeing to administer Scotland in the meantime, although he did not attend the Convention himself. Such a meeting could only be a Convention, since there was as yet no inaugurated king.

Claverhouse, now made Viscount Dundee and loyal to James, returned from England to attend the Convention. The Convention was fairly evenly split between the supporters of the two sides. Both William and James presented letters to the Convention. But while William's letter was moderate and conciliatory, James's was essentially a threat against those that failed in their 'natural allegiance' to the throne and to him. James's letter was not well received, and he alienated many waverers, even Episcopalians, into thinking he might be going to restore the authority of the Pope. The Convention was now decided; divided into a few committed Jacobites, led by Claverhouse; and a much larger number who supported William. They may have been helped in their decision by the presence of an armed force at Leith, led by Mac-Kay of Scourie, supporting William.

Learning of Jacobite support in the Highlands, Claverhouse – who was outlawed by

Claypotts, Dundee – castle of John Graham of Claverhouse.

the Convention in Edinburgh on 30 March – went north. He raised the standard on Dundee Law, but finding little support, headed into the Highlands.

On 4 April 1689 the Estates issued a 'Declaration' comprising a claim of right and an offer of the throne to William of Orange and Mary. The Claim of Right stated that James had 'for-faulted' or forfeited his right as king, and the throne was therefore vacant. It also spelt out some fundamental conditions: that only a Protestant could be monarch, there was to be no taxation without the consent of parliament, and the monarch could not be above the laws of the country. The Articles of Grievances condemned the whole organisation of the previous administration. A new Coronation Oath was also drawn up, and as a result William and Mary were offered the throne provided they upheld the laws, religion and liberties of the Scottish people.

William, at Whitehall in the south of England, agreed to the Declaration, and took the Oath on 11 May 1689, confirming both himself and Mary as joint monarchs. The throne was to go to Anne, James's daughter and Mary's sister, if Mary should die without issue.

The scene was set for the first Jacobite Rising.

4–The 1689 Jacobite Rising

After William and Mary were confirmed as joint monarchs in 1689, the supporters of James VII, then his son, James Francis Edward Stewart 'the Old Pretender', were known as Jacobites. The word comes from the Latin for James – *Jacobus* – but is also said to have been pejorative. In the Bible, Jacob tricked his father Isaac into giving him a blessing meant for his brother. This was apparently a reference to the creative, but unlikely, invention that the infant 'Old Pretender' was not actually the son of James VII and Mary of Modena – and they had no heir to continue the dynasty. The baby, it was claimed, had been smuggled into the Mary's chamber in a warming pan.

James VIII and III (1701) by François de Troy (SNPG).

'Old Pretender' is from the French *pretendant*, meaning claimant. In Scotland there was some loyalty to the Stewarts, and – because of an abiding dislike of the southern neighbour – particularly a Stewart king seemingly harried out of the country by the English.

Jacobite ambitions were not restricted to Scotland, and James VII, his son James Francis Edward, and his grandson Charles Edward 'the Young Pretender', were as keen – if not more so – to regain the English throne, seeing Scotland largely as a stepping stone to secure the southern realm. After all, England was one of the foremost powers in Europe. It should also be remembered that Charles II never visited Scotland after the Restoration in 1660, and that James, himself, showed little more interest in his northern realm, having spent only a few years in Scotland. Mary, James's daughter, continued the family tradition, and William was mostly concerned with preserving his own country, Holland, from the French.

Scotland was a poor country at the end of the 17th century, the economy and agriculture stunted by decades of war. Roads were rough and transport by land difficult, and the growth of trade was restricted by a lack of shipping and properly developed harbours. The situation was made worse by the English Navigation Act of 1661, which restricted Scottish trading with England. Towns such as Edinburgh and Dundee were overcrowded, rife with disease and stinking with raw sewage.

Lowland areas had particularly suffered during the religious troubles, while the Highlands, often seen as lawless and barbaric by the 'peaceful' and 'sophisticated' Lowlander, had been largely left to manage their own affairs.

The Highlands and Lowlands were separated by more than geography: Lowland areas had more in common with England. The Highlanders spoke Gaelic rather than English, their dress and traditions were distinct, such as the wearing of plaid and the playing of bagpipes, and clan organisation was paternalistic and militaristic. This is not to say that the Highlands were in any way less cultured or advanced than the Lowlands, only that it was seen that way in the Lowlands.

The Lowlands were also predominantly Protestant, while there were still areas of the Highlands which were Roman Catholic – or at least Episcopalian.

John Graham of Claverhouse, Viscount Dundee, had gone north to rally support for James. Claverhouse, as James's Lieutenant General, raised an army, mostly composed of MacDonalds, Camerons, Stewarts and MacLeans. They raided Perth on 10 May 1689. Among the army was the 18-year-old Rob Roy MacGregor, renowned for his skill with the broadsword.

The Jacobites had seized the strategically important Blair Castle. Claverhouse learned that a government army, led by General Hugh MacKay of Scourie, was marching from Stirling to recover Blair, and then garrison the fort at Inverlochy. The Jacobites, with about 2000 or so men, moved

John Graham of Claverhouse, Viscount or 'Bonnie' Dundee, also known as 'Bloody Clavers' from his days in Galloway (SNPG).

from their camp at Glen Roy, through the Drumochter Pass, and camped near Blair on 26 July. MacKay reached Dunkeld that night, with 4000 infantry, two cavalry troops, and three old artillery pieces.

The next day MacKay advanced through the narrow Pass of Killiecrankie towards Blair, but found the Jacobites were waiting for him.

MacKay's army was sent uphill through woods, but was overlooked by the Jacobites on a higher ridge. For two hours the two forces faced each other, the government artillery firing on the Jacobites, reportedly only managing to get nine shots off; Claverhouse waiting for evening and the setting sun. Around 7.00pm the Jacobites were ordered to charge. MacKay's men fired, doing much damage to the Highlanders, but the charge was not checked. Much of the government army was then swept away and routed in the fierce

Killiecrankie – the battle took place near here.

onslaught, and the Jacobites overwhelmed the baggage train. The pass was choked with fleeing men.

MacKay made a last stand. Claverhouse led the attack, but was wounded by a musket-ball in the stomach; his men were driven off and could not come to him, and he is said to have been slain by a looter as he lay wounded.

Claverhouse's body was taken to Blair Castle to be buried in the nearby churchyard of old St Bride's. MacKay's younger brother was also killed; and casualties were heavy on both sides. MacKay then rallied 400 of his men and led them southwards towards Weem; by 10 August he was at Aberdeen with a new army.

The victorious Jacobites, now led by an Irish professional soldier Colonel Cannon and their numbers swollen by new recruits, descended on Dunkeld. The town was held by 1200 Cameronians, within the walls of the old cathedral precinct. Much of the town was burnt in the ensuing bitter battle, and losses were heavy on both sides. And although William Clelland, the young Colonel of the Cameronians, was slain, the Jacobites could not take the town and eventually withdrew and disbanded, marauding through the Campbell lands of Breadalbane as they retreated.

The Rising was not quite over. On 1 May 1690 a Jacobite force of about 800 men, led by Major General Thomas Buchan, was encamped in Cromdale. At nearby Castle Grant, a government army led by Sir Thomas Livingstone, learned of the Jacobites' location. Although tired by a day's march, Livingstone attacked the Jacobites that same night, who – unprepared and half-asleep – were routed with the loss of 300 men.

This effectively ended the Jacobite Rising in Scotland, and MacKay strengthened and enlarged the fort at Inverlochy – first built for Cromwell in the 1650s – renaming it Fort William after the new king.

James, meanwhile, had sent word that he would raise Roman Catholic troops in Ireland, and bring them to Scotland, in preparation for an attack on England. William sailed for Ireland with an army, and attacked James at the Battle of the Boyne in 1690. William defeated the Jacobite army easily, and James was forced to return to exile in France.

William had been reluctant to redress the Grievances, particularly the issue of royal supremacy over the Church. By May 1690 he had finally given in, the result being that the Scottish Parliament was free of royal interference. The Parliament of 7 June 1690 abolished Episcopacy and restored a Presbyterian church.

The Scots, however, found that William was little better than the Stewart kings, and he was becoming increasingly unpopular. The Jacobites were still active; the Episcopalians resented the establishment of the Presbyterian church, and many were themselves now being persecuted; the Cameronians were angry as William disregarded parts of the Covenant; and disappointed politicians, some who had not secured as high an office as they felt they deserved, gathered themselves together into the 'Country Party'. In 1691 William appointed Sir John Dalrymple, Master of Stair, as Joint Secretary of State in Edinburgh. Stair had been made Lord Advocate under James VII, but was appointed by William to the same post in 1689, then to Joint Secretary.

William had other cares and was involved in the wars in the Low Countries against the French. Louis XIV of France, meantime, had recognised the exiled James VII as King of Scotland, England and Ireland. Yet dissent rumbled on. In 1692 William dismissed the

General Assembly of the Church, which he feared would cause him more trouble, without arranging a date for their next meeting.

Although James VII continued to plan, plot and scheme to recover his kingdom from exile in France, his attempts floundered and in the end came to nothing. Louis XIV of France was reluctant to spend money and resources on James's plans, while Jacobite support in Scotland and England was so uncertain. Yet the cause did not die. In Scotland there were still many who regarded James as their rightful king, or felt disaffected enough with William and Mary to support the Jacobites. The passage of time also dulled the memory, many forgetting their dislike and distrust of James.

Many clans, like the MacLeans and Camerons, saw the Jacobites as a means of asserting themselves against the powerful Campbell Earls of Argyll, who supported William of Orange and had been encroaching on their lands. Besides, parts of the Highlands were poor and lawless, the main offenders said to have been the MacLeans, Camerons, MacDonalds, MacLachlans and the MacGregors, and the extortion of blackmail and the thieving of cattle was not uncommon – these were often desperate times.

The Jacobite cause was further strengthened, ironically, by the actions of William and his government for their part in the Massacre of Glencoe and in the Darien Scheme.

5–The Massacre of Glencoe and the Darien Scheme

Although the Jacobites had failed for now, the government was concerned about how easy it had been for Claverhouse – and others before him – to raise men from the Highlands: Claverhouse had assembled a large and effective army, which might have given William of Orange real problems. It certainly drained resources which William could have used against the French. The government was faced with the problem of trying to pacify the powerful clans, while a shortage of resources ruled out a full-scale military campaign. It was also recognised that poverty in the Highlands was one of the causes of unrest and disorder.

The government decided to use bribery to buy the clans' allegiance. Under the direction of Stair, John Campbell, Earl of Breadalbane, was given monies with which he came to an arrangement with many Jacobite chiefs at Achallader, although he reportedly kept much of the money for himself. The Jacobite clans agreed to an armistice and accepted the financial compensation, but they wanted time to seek James VII's approval.

Stair became frustrated with the time it was all taking, and in August 1691 a new strategy was devised: the government promised

Glencoe – the massacre took place here in 1692.

an amnesty to all those who took an oath of allegiance to William and Mary before 1 January 1692. This policy was designed to snare any recalcitrant Jacobite clans, as dire retribution was to be brought against any who failed to take the oath. After much hesitation, nearly all did: James VII and II tacitly agreed they should do so. MacLean of Duart and MacDonald of Glengarry refused, but both had strong castles and were too powerful to be singled out for punishment.

MacIain of Glencoe, chief of a small branch of the large and powerful Clan Donald, was just what Stair wanted. MacIain set out to take the oath, but went in the wrong direction. He arrived at Fort William on 31 December 1691 – in time – but Colonel Hill, Governor of the garrison, was not empowered to take the oath. After a difficult journey back south through snow, MacIain reached Inveraray, the correct destination, but it was already 2 January. There were further delays, but Campbell of Ardkinglas, the Sheriff, did in fact accept MacIain's oath on the 6 January – the further delay is said to have been caused by Campbell's hangover from New Year celebrations. When the news of MacIain's late arrival reached Edinburgh, however, the oath was rejected.

The MacDonalds of Glencoe were ideal as a target for punishment; they lived in an area from which there was no easy escape; they were staunch supporters of James VII, although it would

Inveraray Castle – it was at an earlier building that MacIain of Glencoe took the Oath, but it was rejected by the government and the Massacre of Glencoe followed.

appear they were Episcopalians rather than Roman Catholics; and they were reputedly a lawless lot, whose thievery of their neighbours' property, albeit in difficult and troubled times, had made them particularly unpopular.

Organised by Stair, orders were passed to Sir Thomas Livingstone, Commander-in-Chief in Scotland. Before they were passed down the line of command, they were signed by William of Orange. Orders to Colonel Hill at Fort William were clear: no mercy was to be shown to the MacDonalds of Glencoe.

On 1 February 1692 the Campbell Earl of Argyll's Regiment was moved into Glencoe and billeted on the MacDonalds. The MacDonalds had not paid their taxes, and were liable for the quartering of government soldiers.

Captain Robert Campbell of Glenlyon, a 60-year-old alcoholic who had been ruined – at least in part – by the MacDonalds of Glencoe plundering of his lands, led the party. His orders were that all men of the clan under 70 were to be slain.

At dawn on 13 February the massacre began. MacIain, his wife, two of his sons and a number of the clan, about 38 in total, were killed by government soldiers or in the aftermath trying to flee. The massacre, nevertheless, was badly executed – probably deliberately so. Many of the MacDonalds escaped from the glen, although others died in the snow of the passes, and found refuge with the Stewarts of Appin to the south and west of Glencoe.

The consequences of the massacre were not as anticipated by Stair and the government. They had handed the Jacobites a propaganda victory, and a storm of criticism rose, directed at all those involved, from the troops on the ground right up to William. Criticism was even levelled from the Lowlands, where normally Highlanders were scorned and feared. The cruel and treacherous act, far from cowing the Highlands, in the long run greatly increased support for the Jacobites.

The massacre was not, as is sometimes thought, a clan feud between the MacDonalds and the Campbells – although there was bad blood between the two clans. It was, also, by no means the most vicious act in Highland history: the MacDonalds burned a congregation of MacLeods to death in a church at Trumpan on Skye;

while islanders on Rum were suffocated when the cave in which they were sheltering was blocked up and the barricade set on fire. It was, however, a deliberate and ruthless action, with full government sanction right up to William, to punish the MacDonalds of Glencoe and make an example of them. In this it certainly failed and their policy backfired. In 1695 Stair was forced to resign as Secretary of State, the same year as he became Viscount Stair. It was the only punishment to result from the massacre: no proper investigation was ever made.

Stair did not do all that badly: in 1703 Queen Anne made him Earl of Stair.

Another series of events which increased William's unpopularity was the Darien Scheme.

The enterprise began when in 1695 Scottish Parliament passed an Act for the establishment of a 'company of Scotland trading to Africa and the Indies'. There was some support from William, although this remained vague, and was probably designed to distract attention from the repercussions of the Massacre of Glencoe.

The idea behind the company was to increase trade to and from Scotland – the Scots were barred from English colonies, although there was some illicit trade and smuggling. The ban was a result of the English Navigation Act of 1661, which restricted goods brought into England to English vessels or ships of the country of origin. Small Scottish trading posts had been established in New Jersey, and at Stuart's Town in South Carolina, but these had been largely unsuccessful.

The Scots modelled the new company 'The Company of Scotland' on the very successful English East India Company, granting it similar privileges. It was to be a joint enterprise with the English. Half the capital was to be raised in London, and the company was to be managed from London.

Enthusiasm was rife and £300 000 was raised in two weeks, but support quickly evaporated when the English House of Commons threatened to impeach the directors: many English merchants saw the Scottish company as a threat to their economic interests. The East India Company was to keep its monopoly, and the Scottish company was left to struggle on without official support. William, indeed, was now actively hostile, blocking the borrowing of money and the purchasing of ships.

Opposition by the English encouraged the Scots into a flurry of fund raising, and they managed to raise capital of £400 000. On 12 July 1698 three ships and two smaller vessels set sail from Leith, for Darien on the isthmus of Panama, although the destination was kept secret until they arrived at Madeira. Darien had been chosen because of supposed ease of access to trade with the Americas, and for avoiding the long sea routes to the east.

The presence of the Spanish at Cartagena in Columbia, on the other side of the isthmus, had been ignored; as had disease – and, of course, the fact there was no canal meant there was great difficulty in transporting goods across the jungle and broken ground of the narrow isthmus.

The ships arrived on 3 November at a sheltered spot called Acla, which was renamed Caledonia, and the colonists built a small settlement, called New Edinburgh, and Fort St Andrew.

The Scots, however, found themselves between the English in Jamaica to the north, and the Spanish to the south.

The English were prohibited by Royal proclamation from trading with the Scots – William did not wish to antagonise the Spanish – while the Spanish, who claimed the area, were preparing to attack the new settlement.

There was a small battle in February 1699, when the Spanish were defeated, but the situation in the settlement was deteriorating: supplies were low, desertions and disease were common, and English and Spanish hostility was growing – and the whole enterprise was badly managed and organised.

In June the colonists abandoned the settlement, and set out on the return voyage. None of the ships got back to Leith: one was unseaworthy; a second was abandoned in Jamaica; the third in New York. Of the 1200 Scots, 900 survived the occupation of Darien, but a further 150 died on the voyage. Few ever returned to Scotland.

The settlement had been abandoned shortly before a second party arrived, but this party only stayed from November 1699 to March 1700. A combined force of Scots and Indians easily defeated a Spanish attack, but the colonists were again poorly supplied, and when the Spanish besieged the settlement and captured Fort St Andrew, the Scots surrendered on honourable terms.

Scotland had lost 2000 men and upwards of £200 000, and much anger was directed against William and the English, some translating to support for the Jacobites. The scheme left Scotland in serious economic difficulties, not helped by several poor harvests at home. Many Scottish troops were also being raised to fight in William's wars with the French, and this led to further resentment.

The company, meanwhile, survived for another seven years, and attempted to trade in the East, culminating in acts of piracy between the Scots and the East India Company. In Edinburgh the innocent English sea captain of the *Worcester* and some of his men were hanged and their vessel seized.

This contributed to the less than harmonious atmosphere between the two nations at the time, and the situation was never properly resolved until the company was wound up as part of the Act of Union – which was supposed to include compensation, with interest, for all those who had invested in the scheme.

Besides, patriotic amnesia resulted in many forgetting to blame their fellow Scots for the chronic mismanagement of the scheme.

6–The Treaty of Union 1707

A combination of circumstances contributed to what has been seen as the inevitability of the Union of the Parliaments of Scotland and England. First were the consequences of the Darien Scheme, which demonstrated the difficulty of Scotland trading with English colonies, or setting up colonies in opposition to England. Union would give Scotland increased trade and greater wealth. The English saw the benefit of the abolition of the often independently minded Scottish Parliament, reducing the likelihood of dispute over foreign policy and wars. There was also the question of the succession, as Anne's only surviving child died in 1700.

James VII, himself, turned with increasing devotion to Roman Catholicism in the last years of his life. Having acquired something of a reputation as a holy man, on his death in 1701 his body was dismembered and further cut up, parts being given to different institutions.

The same year the English Parliament passed an Act of Settlement, offering the Crown to the heirs of Sophia of Hanover, daughter of Elizabeth of Bohemia the Winter Queen, herself a daughter of James VI and I. The Scottish Parliament was not consulted, and this act of arrogance again angered the northern realm. There was a real possibility that the Scottish Parliament would not accept the Act of Settlement – it was not obliged to do so – and would chose James Francis Edward 'the Old Pretender', son of James VII, as their next monarch, should he have converted to Protestantism – although there was never any question he would.

William of Orange died on 8 March 1702, his horse tripping on a mole hill in the grounds of Hampton Court and throwing him; although his injuries did not appear to be serious, he died of pleurisy. The Jacobites afterwards toasted the 'little gentleman in black velvet jacket': the mole that had dug the hole. Mary had died of smallpox in 1694, at the age of only 32, and the couple were childless: William, it has been said by some, preferred the company of boys, although he is also said to have had several mistresses. William never once visited his northern kingdom.

Family Tree of Kings of Scots, England and Britain (1567-1830)

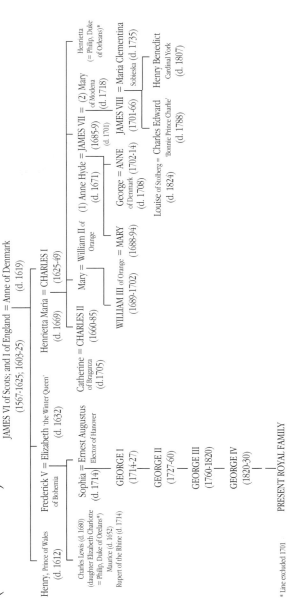

JAMES VI of Scots; and I of England = Anne of Denmark (1567-1625; 1603-25) (d. 1619)

Henry, Prince of Wales (d. 1612)

Frederick V = Elizabeth 'the Winter Queen' of Bohemia (d. 1632)

Henrietta Maria = CHARLES I (d. 1669) (1625-49)

Charles Lewis (d. 1680)
(daughter Elizabeth Charlotte = Philip, Duke of Orelans*)
Maurice (d. 1652)
Rupert of the Rhine (d. 1714)

Sophia = Ernest Augustus (d. 1714) Elector of Hanover

GEORGE I (1714-27)

GEORGE II (1727-60)

GEORGE III (1760-1820)

GEORGE IV (1820-30)

PRESENT ROYAL FAMILY

Catherine = CHARLES II of Braganza (1660-85) (d. 1705)

Mary, = William II of Orange

WILLIAM III of Orange = MARY (1689-1702) (1688-94)

(1) Anne Hyde = JAMES VII = (2) Mary (d. 1671) (1685-9) of Modena (d. 1701) (d. 1718)

George = ANNE of Denmark (1702-14) (d. 1708)

JAMES VIII = Maria Clementina (1701-66) Sobieska (d. 1735)

Louise of Stolberg = Charles Edward 'Bonnie Prince Charlie' (d. 1824) (d. 1788)

Henry Benedict Cardinal York (d. 1807)

Henrietta (= Philip, Duke of Orleans)*

* Line excluded 1701

Anne, younger daughter of James VII and Anne Hyde, came to the throne in 1702. She was more popular than William, free from the mire of the Massacre of Glencoe and the Darien Scheme. Although she reintroduced the *Order of the Thistle* in 1703, she never visited Scotland as Queen.

As an Episcopalian and Anglican, she could not accept the claim of her half-brother James 'the Old Pretender', who was staunchly Roman Catholic. Within two months of her coming to the throne in 1702, war had been declared on France – the War of the Spanish Succession – fought upon the death of Charles II of Spain, the last Spanish Hapsburg monarch.

That same year James Douglas, 2nd Duke of Queensberry, Anne's Secretary of State for Scotland, managed to push a bill through the Scottish Parliament nominating Commissioners to discuss the possibility of a Union of Parliaments. Nothing came of this first proposal.

Queensberry and the pro-Union faction were then wrong-footed, as in 1703 the Scottish Parliament passed the Act Anent Peace and War, rejecting the costly war with France, and affirming the right of the Scottish Parliament to decide whether or not to get involved in foreign wars after the death of Anne. In 1704 the Act of Security was passed by the Scottish Parliament, which threw the Hanoverian settlement into question, and proposed that Scotland had the right to make its own decision about the succession, selecting a descendant of the Stewart monarchs as long as they were Protestant.

The English were increasingly concerned about French support for the Jacobites, and began to see Union as a means of getting its northern neighbour into line, preventing Scotland from ever again supporting their enemies. In 1705 the English Parliament passed the Alien Act, which gave the Scots ten months to repeal the Act of Security, and accept the Hanoverian settlement, or start negotiations for Union. If this was not done, the Scots would lose the right to English citizenship – they would become 'aliens' – which had been negotiated by James VI, and duty-free trade of cattle, linen and coal was to be abolished. The English fleet would blockade ports, and prevent the Scots trading with the Continent, as was already the case with English colonies.

Commissioners were subsequently appointed on both sides to discuss terms for the Union.

In the early stages, a majority of Scottish MPs from the anti-Unionist 'Country Party', headed by James Hamilton 4th Duke of Hamilton, and then by Alexander Fletcher of Saltoun after Hamilton's turning, were opposed to Union. They were the largest group in Parliament, but they offered no workable alternative to the increasingly strong economic arguments of those who favoured the Union. They were made up of a mixed band of Jacobites, Presbyterians, Episcopalians, nobles who had been unsuccessful in securing high office in the government, discontented Darien investors, and a few Parliamentarians, such as Fletcher. This disparate group was easily divided as their aims were entirely different.

The Court Party was in favour of the Union, and a third group, the New Party or *squadroni volante*, led by John Hay, 2nd Marquis of Tweeddale, were initially neutral, although subsequently supported the Court Party. Hamilton unexpectedly came out in favour of the Union, despite having been strongly opposed to it – he may have received a large amount of money, and been promised more – and Queen Anne selected Commissioners who were, on the whole, predisposed to the Treaty. Queensberry and the Lord Chancellor James Ogilvie, Earl of Seafield; then later John Campbell, 2nd Duke of Argyll, and John Erskine, 6th Earl of Mar, skilfully manipulated the parties to Anne's advantage.

There were 25 articles in the Treaty of Union. Alternative federal proposals which had been suggested by others, notably Fletcher and John Hamilton, 2nd Lord Belhaven, had all been rejected. It should be said that neither of the men were Jacobites: they had opposed James VII and welcomed William and Mary onto the throne. They would have done well out of the Union as they had both invested in the Darien scheme.

The Union was one of incorporation, not federation. There was to be one parliament, one monarch of the Hanoverian line after Anne should she have no suitable heirs, one flag, one coinage, one system of weights and measures, one Great Seal, one system of tax, and unified trading regulations with free access for Scottish merchants to England's colonies. Scotland was to be allowed to keep a separate legal system and Church. There was much debate about the number of seats Scotland was to be given in the united parliament, and the figure eventually reached was 42 in a House of Commons of 558 members, and only 16 in the House of Lords.

Scotland was also to get some recompense for the Darien Scheme, investors were to be reimbursed after the 'Company of Scotland' was wound up. £2000 a year was also pledged to help Scottish industries.

When the draft Treaty was presented to the Scottish Parliament in October 1706, and when the conditions became generally known, there was a general feeling that Scotland had been sold to the English – *bought and sold for English gold* – and there were riots in Edinburgh, Dumfries and Glasgow. Nevertheless, the Scottish Parliament passed the first of these Articles in November 1706, and the final vote was carried through by 110 to 67 on 16 January 1707, despite much opposition by the general populace. The Scottish Parliament was dissolved in April, and the Union of the Parliaments of Scotland and England became official on 1 May 1707, when the new Parliament of Great Britain came into being.

Queensberry was rewarded for his part in helping establish the Union: besides his current office and titles, he was made Duke of Dover, Marquess of Beverley and Earl of Ripon. Hamilton also got a Dukedom, being created Duke of Brandon in 1711, but was killed in duel a year later. Argyll obtained an earldom for his brother, and was made a field marshal. Seafield, however, later urged the repealing of the Union, and his motion only failed by four proxy votes. Fletcher retired from politics after 1707 to concentrate on agrarian reform.

There was still much resentment and discomfort over the Treaty, but it had been hard to ignore the threat of the Alien Act – war or economic hardship – and the large sums of money available in bribes.

The English, however, hardly improved matters: many acted as if Scotland had been absorbed into England, and the provisions of the Treaty of Union were often ignored, not least recompense for the Darien Scheme.

Map 2: Scotland 1707-45

7–The 1715 and 1719 Jacobite Risings

The only surviving son of James VII and Mary of Modena, James Francis Edward 'the Old Pretender' was born in St James's Palace, London in 1688. He was made Prince of Wales by his father and, on his father's death in 1701, was proclaimed King of England, Scotland and Ireland at St Germain in France, 'James VIII of Scots and III of England'. The title was recognised by France and Spain, although it was contrary to the Act of Succession in England.

Linlithgow Palace – Anne stayed here with James VII, when he was Duke of York.

James VII had died in September 1701, William in 1702, and Anne, daughter of James VII and Anne Hyde, was now on the throne, having been recognised by the Scottish Parliament. She was married at 18 to Prince George of Denmark, 12 years her senior, and although she had many pregnancies, none of her children survived into adulthood. Anne visited Scotland once with her father in 1682, and is said to have been horrified by James's cruel persecution of the Covenanters. Perhaps because of this, and the constant trouble between the two kingdoms, Anne was determined to see the two countries united under one Parliament, and this she had achieved in 1707.

In Scotland resentment rumbled on over the Treaty of Union and led to increased support for the Jacobites. Meanwhile, Louis XIV of France was at war with the English over the Spanish Succession, and was happy to support the Jacobite cause – and cause as much trouble for the English as possible. In 1705 opinion was sounded out in Scotland about the return of James VIII, and although reaction was favourable, indeed probably overly optimistic, there was to be much delay. A letter asking for French support promised that the whole Scottish nation was ready to rise as soon as James landed. Louis XIV responded by organising a small fleet which sailed from Dunkirk in 1708 with James aboard.

The voyage was rough, and the 19-year-old 'Old Pretender' suffered from sea sickness; he was also recovering from a bout of measles. The fleet reached the Firth of Forth, but bad weather and the arrival of a large fleet of English ships aborted plans to disembark at Burntisland. The fleet sailed north, James vainly pleading to be put ashore, then finally returned to France, arriving back at Dunkirk on 7 April. The Rising had failed without even landing on dry ground.

In 1708-9 James fought with the French forces at Malplaquet and Oudenarde, gaining a reputation for bravery. A proposed French invasion of 1710 came to nothing. By 1713, however, the War of the Spanish Succession was over, and with the Peace of Utrecht, Louis XIV agreed to expel James from France. James moved to Bar-le-Duc in Lorraine.

James had been beset by ill-luck – even the weather seemed to conspire to thwart him and one of his nicknames was 'old Mr Misfortune' – but another opportunity to regain the throne arose on the death of Anne, and the succession of the German George I. George was the first of the Hanoverian monarchs, but could not speak English, and was, indeed, reluctant to leave Germany .

Anne had died in 1714. Resentment against the Union had not diminished: it had not brought the expected economic benefits, the position aggravated by several dire harvests. The English had made matters worse by imposing taxation on Scotland, which further damaged already weak Scottish industries. Added to this was the succession of George I, which few in Scotland welcomed.

All this left many Scots believing that their once proud nation had become little more than a grubby and limp appendage of England.

John Erskine, 6th Earl of Mar, was Secretary of State for Scotland under Anne, and held the post when she died. He was one of the Commissioners and a staunch supporter of the Act of Union. George I, however, deprived Mar of his office and offered him nothing as recompense. Mar was angered by this, and returned to Scotland. Known as 'Bobbing John' for the frequency and fervour with which he had changed sides, Erskine was worried he might be arrested, and went to north to his castle at Braemar. There he raised the standard for James VIII and III 'the Old Pretender' on 16 September 1715, and declared himself a Jacobite.

John Erskine, Earl of Mar, studio of Sir Geoffrey Kneller (SNPG).

His timing was unfortunate: Louis XIV of France had died five days earlier and James VIII was on the other side of Europe. Word of the Rising was enough to bring James to Dunkirk, this time in disguise, from where he sailed for Scotland, although he had been delayed for several months, a delay which was to prove costly.

There was much alarm among the Hanoverian government, and John Campbell, 2nd Duke of Argyll, one of the supporters of the Union, was appointed Commander-in-Chief in Scotland. Argyll rallied Hanoverian forces to oppose Mar, but could only raise a modest force. He believed that nine out of ten Scots would support the rising, although not because they were Jacobites, rather because of the unpopularity of George I and the English. In England, after all, there was also disenchantment with the Hanoverian government, and sympathy for the Jacobite cause.

Mar managed to raise an army of about 12 000 men, some say 20 000 men, including important nobles such as the Keith Earl Marischal and the Gordon Earl of Huntly, as well as clans such as the MacLeans, Mackenzies, MacRaes. MacDonalds, MacGregors, Camerons and Mackintoshes.

But there was no aid from France, and no rising in the south of England to help them. The Jacobites sent a force under Gordon of Auchintoul to take Fort William; the Master of Caithness was sent south to occupy Fife; while Mar and the main part of the army marched south; Mackintosh of Borlum took Inverness on 14 September.

By November the Jacobites had reached and captured Perth, but here Mar hesitated.

Argyll had managed to raise an army of 4000 men to block Mar's advance south. The Jacobites sent a force of 1500 men, under Mackintosh of Borlum, through Fife from where they crossed into East Lothian via North Berwick and seized Haddington. Mackintosh advanced on Edinburgh but, worried that the castle was too strong to capture, occupied Leith. Argyll refortified Edinburgh, but led the main part of his army to Stirling. Mar had now advanced as far as Dunblane, and battle became inevitable.

The two armies met on 13 November at Sheriffmuir, near Dunblane, and although Mar outnumbered Argyll by over two to one, the battle was indecisive.

The right flank of the Jacobites, led by MacDonald of Glengarry, MacLean of Duart, and MacDonald of Clan Ranald routed the left side of the Hanoverian army. Argyll and a force of dragoons, however, attacked the Jacobite right and drove them back with much slaughter. Neither side wished to pursue the battle, and both withdrew. Mar retreated to Perth, and Argyll to Dunblane.

Among those at the battle was Rob Roy MacGregor, and although he took no part in the fighting, he was outlawed for treason, and his home was burnt by government troops.

Although both sides then claimed victory, it was the Jacobites who were to suffer. Mar's failure to crush Argyll, despite the fact he had a much larger army, was bad propaganda: the French and Spanish were reluctant to support what appeared to be a failing cause.

Inverness, meanwhile, was retaken for the Hanoverians by Simon Fraser of Lovat.

Worse news was to follow as a Jacobite army of Scottish Lowlanders, led by the Gordon Viscount Kenmure and the Maxwell Earl of Nithsdale; a force of Roman Catholic Northumbrian gentry under the Earl of Derwentwater; and Mackintosh of Borlum with a depleted force of Highlanders were defeated at the Battle of Preston in the north of England. The Jacobites fought bravely, barricaded within the town, but they were greatly outnumbered and were forced to surrender on 14 November. Mackintosh of Borlum later escaped to fight another day.

Then, early in December, the Hanoverian army was reinforced by 6000 Dutch troops from the Continent.

When James VIII and III landed at Peterhead, in December, the cause was all but lost. James held 'court' at Scone, and Jacobite ladies were persuaded to hand over their jewels for making into a crown. James was to spend six weeks in Scotland, but got no further south than Perth before withdrawing up the east coast – as his army dwindled and disbanded, sated with plunder. James boarded ship at Montrose in February 1716, and went back to France, the leaders of the Rising either accompanying him or following him, including the Earl of Mar. They reached France on 10 February.

Mar's estates and lands were forfeited, and although he appeared to support the Jacobites in exile, there was some question as to whether he was a spy for the Hanoverian government. Whatever, he later abandoned the Jacobite cause, but died in exile at Aix-la-Chapelle in France.

The suppression of the Rising was mild compared with what was to come some 20 years later. Nineteen Scots and two English peers lost their estates. Eight noblemen were condemned to death, but only

Derwentwater and Kenmure were actually executed, while 22 of the army taken at Preston were hanged, and hundreds of others transported. The Disarming Act was introduced – an attempt to get the Highlanders to hand in their broadswords, axes and muskets – but this was largely unsuccessful and the weapons were only hidden. Juries refused to prosecute 'absent' Jacobites, and there was widespread sympathy for the political motives of the Rising. The government was persuaded against extreme measures.

In 1717 an Act of Grace pardoned all rebels, except the MacGregors. The government had also made virtually nothing from the forfeited estates, an indication of both the poverty of the Jacobite landowners, and their own mismanagement.

James VIII returned to Lorraine, then in 1717 went to Rome, and entered into negotiations with Charles XII of Sweden, who had his own quarrel with the Hanoverians; but Charles was killed before anything could come of the plan.

James was invited to Spain in 1719 – there was new found support from the Spanish government of Philip V – to head a force organised by Cardinal Aleroni, the Spanish foreign minister, to invade England. The invading fleet, however, was wrecked in storms in the Bay of

Eilean Donan Castle – see next page.

Biscay, and only the diversionary party actually managed to arrive in Scotland.

About 300 Spanish troops and Jacobites under George Keith, 9th Earl Marischal; William Murray, Marquis of Tullibardine; Mackintosh of Borlum; and the Mackenzie Earl of Seaforth landed from two Spanish ships in Kintail. They joined forces with Cameron of Lochiel, Lord George Murray, and Rob Roy MacGregor, and together they mustered about 1000 men. They quickly seized Eilean Donan Castle, and garrisoned it as a supply base.

In June a Hanoverian force of 1600 men under General Wightman approached from Inverness. Eilean Donan Castle was bombarded into submission by three Hanoverian frigates, and the magazine was then detonated from within, destroying much of the castle. A battle followed at nearby Glen Shiel on 10 September, but while casualties were about even, the Jacobites' morale was low and they disbanded. The Spaniards, most of whom appear to have survived the battle, surrendered, were held as prisoners of war, and eventually returned home. The Jacobite leaders found their own way back to the continent through the Highlands.

Again, it seemed, bad luck had ruined the Stewart cause.

8–Bonnie Prince Charlie

Measures had been taken to subdue the Highlands, such as the Disarming Act, but were largely ineffective. Other measures included the creation and maintenance of Hanoverian garrisons at Bernera, Inversnaid, Ruthven, Inverness and Kilchurn, while there were forts

Kilchurn Castle

at Fort William and Fort Augustus. The building of military roads to connect these points was overseen by General George Wade, who built 240 miles of roads with 40 bridges. Wade, an Irishman, served in Flanders between 1692 and 1710, was made a Major General in 1714, and from 1724 until 1744 was Commander-in-Chief North Britain. One outcome of his new roads was, paradoxically, the speedy transit of Jacobite forces.

Incidentally, Wade has the honour of being referred to in the National Anthem. One verse hopes that General Wade will 'like a torrent rush, rebellious Scots to crush', and that he will 'confound their politics, frustrate their knavish tricks'.

Despite these measures, discontent rumbled on, not the least because of the chronic maladministration of Scotland by the government, and the disinterest shown by the Hanoverian monarchs in the northern part of their kingdom.

The Malt Tax was raised in 1724 – a tax on beer – causing riots in Glasgow and Edinburgh, as well it might, and the house of Daniel Campbell of Shawfield, who was said to have supported the tax, was plundered and razed.

Further unrest followed in 1736 with the imposition of a new customs and excise system, as smuggling was widespread. This culminated in Edinburgh with the Porteous Riot, where the captain of the city guard, John Porteous, was hanged by a mob. He had presided at the execution of a smuggler, and then opened fire on angry spectators. It should be said, however, that neither Edinburgh nor Glasgow showed much support for the Jacobites. There was general acceptance of the Union in the Lowlands, and there had been some improvements in agriculture and in the Scottish economy in general.

Rob Roy MacGregor, meantime, submitted to General Wade in 1725 and was pardoned. He died peacefully on 31 January 1734 near Balquhidder.

James VIII and III, meanwhile, had withdrawn from Spain and, finding support from the Papacy, settled in Rome. His wedding to the 16-year-old Clementina Sobieski, granddaughter of the King of Poland, in 1719 was a marriage of convenience, but resulted in the birth of Charles Edward in 1720, 'the Young Pretender', and Henry Benedict in 1725. James and Clementina do not appear to have been very happy, and she died in 1735.

The Jacobites were heartened by the birth of Charles as a figurehead to continue the cause. The Prince spoke English, French and Spanish, and is said to have picked up enough Gaelic to make himself understood. He was said to be charming and gifted in conversation – and also to have been able to play the bagpipes. He is also said to have been bisexual, and hence the title 'Bonnie'.

George I died in 1727 and was succeeded by his son, George II, who was no better liked than his father. Britain and France remained at peace, although by 1738 the two countries were once again drifting towards war. Scottish Jacobites formed an Association, and word was sent to France that if the French sent arms, money and a force to guard it, the Jacobites could raise 20 000 men – but this came to nothing.

In 1740 Charles Edward wrote to his father: 'I go, Sire, in search of three crowns, which I do not doubt but to have the honour and

Bonnie Prince Charlie by Antonio David (SNPG).

happiness of laying at your majesty's feet. If I fail in the attempt, your next sight of me will be in my coffin.'

It was not until 1743-4, however, that Louis XV and the French organised another expedition, and assembled a force of 10 000 men with plenty of weapons and money. Having crossed Europe in disguise, Charles joined the party, with orders to act as Regent for his father. The force left Dunkirk, and set sail under the command of Marshal Saxe, but then the inevitable happened: storms forced the ships back to port, and the French hesitated, unwilling to leave again.

By 1745 Charles could wait no longer, and decided to set off in the French ship *Du Teillay*. He pawned his mother's jewels, borrowed more money, and left Nantes in June 1745 with 4000 gold coins, two ships and 700 men. Before he even reached Scotland, one of his vessels was forced to turn back after being attacked by an English warship. The venture had no backing from any European power: he had not even told his father or the French government of his plans. Indeed, the French had won the Battle of Fontenoy in 1745, beating an army led by the Duke of Cumberland, and saw no need to pursue an invasion of Britain.

So it was Bonnie Prince Charlie reached Eriskay, between South Uist and Barra, in the Outer Hebrides on 22 July, and there disembarked from his ship. He was accompanied by only seven companions, one was English, three were Irish, one was a MacDonald from Ulster, as well as Sir Thomas Murray, Marquis of Tullibardine.

The following day, however, brought little cheer: the local chiefs – Alexander MacDonald of Sleat and Norman MacLeod of Dunvegan – advised him to return to France. They had only agreed to back him if he brought sufficient men and supplies to make a realistic challenge to the Hanoverian government – which he manifestly had not. Even the majority of his seven supporters advised abandoning the enterprise; but Charles refused to leave, and persuaded his small force to reboard their ship and make for the Scottish mainland.

Map 3: Scotland 1745-6
also see Map 4 (page 50) and Map 5 (page 55)

ORKNEY

Kirkwall

Thurso

Wick

LEWIS

Stornoway

Ullapool

HARRIS

Dornoch

NORTH UIST

Cullen   Fraserburgh

Elgin   Peterhead

Fort George

BENBECULA   Portree   RAASAY   Inverness   ✕Culloden (1746)

Inverurie

SOUTH UIST   SKYE   Moy   Corgarff Castle   Aberdeen

Fort Augustus

ERISKAY   Bernera   Ruthven   Braemar Castle

BARRA   Invergarry

Corrieyarack Pass   Dalwhinnie

Loch nan Uamh   Glenfinnan   Fort William

Blair Castle

Montrose

Castle Menzies   Dunkeld

MULL   Scone   Dundee

Iona   Oban   Crieff   Perth   St Andrews

Kilchurn   Inveraray

JURA   Edinburgh

Dumbarton   Stirling   Dunbar

ISLAY   Falkirk ✕   Linlithgow   ✕ Prestonpans
(1746)   Dalkeith   (1745)

Glasgow   Hamilton

BUTE   Lauder   Berwick

ARRAN   Traquair

Ayr   Douglas Castle

ENGLAND
Northumberland

Drumlanrig

Dumfries   Hexham

Stranraer   Carlisle

9–The 1745 Jacobite Rising

Bonnie Prince Charlie landed at Loch nan Uamh, southeast of Arisaig on the Scottish mainland, on 25 July 1745, accompanied by his companions, the Seven Men of Moidart. He spent a week at Glenborrodale House, on the south coast of Ardnamurchan, then a further week at Kinlochmoidart in Moidart. Here he was joined by John Murray of Broughton, who the Prince made his secretary. But, although the clans chiefs were reverential – Cameron of Lochiel among them – the advice was the same: Charles should return to France. These men had much to lose, both their lives and their property; and the Prince had brought little in the way of support or supplies. But the Prince was determined to go on, and issued messages to Jacobites leaders that he would raise his father's standard on 19 August at Glenfinnan.

The response at Glenfinnan was hardly dramatic, and for several hours on 19 August the Prince and his supporters waited in the rain, but little support came. It was not until mid-afternoon that 700 Camerons and another 300 or so men under MacDonald of Keppoch finally arrived. The standard was then raised by William

Glenfinnan – the standard was raised here in 1745 for James VIII by Bonnie Prince Charlie.

49

Murray, Marquis of Tullibardine; and James VIII and III was proclaimed king. Charles had managed to raise an army of only about 1000 men, but was lucky that during 1744-5 the Scottish administration, headed by Duncan Forbes of Culloden, Lord President of the Court of Session, had little money – and had themselves only a small untried army of 3000 troops. The Hanoverian government, it seems, did not rate the Jacobites a serious threat. George II, meantime, was on the continent.

Map 4: North-West Scotland 1745-6

As soon as news of Charles's landing reached Edinburgh on 8 August, Forbes sent the Hanoverian army, under Sir John Cope, north towards Fort Augustus. Forbes was determined to crush the Rising before it had time to gather strength.

Cope travelled by Crieff, and had arrived at Dalwhinnie by 26 August, but there he was warned that the Jacobites, said to number some 3000 men although there was probably only half that, held the Corrieyarack Pass. Cope decided not to proceed – probably sensibly – and withdrew to the government barracks at Ruthven. He did not have enough supplies to return to Edinburgh through the Highlands, and made for Inverness and then Aberdeen, where he summoned ships to take his army back to Dunbar.

The way was open for Charles and his army to advance on Edinburgh.

Meanwhile, the Jacobites made full use of the roads General Wade built and marched quickly southwards to Blair Castle – once home of William Murray, Marquis of Tullibardine – and then via Dunkeld to Perth. The town fell without a fight, and here the army stopped for a few days to gather more men, finally numbering about 2000 troops. Charles was taken to Scone to see where so many of his ancestors had been inaugurated as Kings of

Lord George Murray by Sir Robert Strange (SNPG) – see next page.

Scots. Things were going very well and all news was good: there were pledges of support from both the French and the Spanish. Jacobite support was growing, and the Prince had been joined by James Drummond, Duke of Perth; David Wemyss, Lord Elcho; Lord Ogilvie; Laurence Oliphant of Gask; and Lord George Murray, an experienced soldier and able tactician. Murray was appointed Lieutenant General of the Jacobite forces, although only after a squabble with Drummond, who had also been given the same position.

Lord George was the son of the 1st Duke of Atholl and the brother of the Marquis of Tullibardine. After joining the 1715 and 1719 Risings, he went into exile and fought in Sardinia. He was pardoned and returned to Scotland in the 1720s. Lord George was by all accounts a blunt individual, and his manner and tactics came to antagonise both the Prince and his Irish advisors. The Jacobite force was generally well disciplined and organised, and this was mostly due to Murray.

The Jacobites decided to press on and marched towards Edinburgh. They left Perth on 11 September, and crossed the River Forth at Stirling, then went east via Bannockburn and Callendar House, Falkirk, to arrive at Linlithgow Palace on 15 September, where the Prince spent the night. The Jacobites reached Corstorphine, to the west of Edinburgh, the next day, and entered the city on 17 September.

They captured Edinburgh without any real opposition or bloodshed, but could not take the castle on its rock. Although the castle only had a small Hanoverian garrison, its position and strength made it impossible to capture without a difficult siege.

Charles was welcomed into the city by cheering crowds, and James VIII and III was proclaimed king at the market cross. The Prince made Holyroodhouse, at the foot of the Royal Mile in Edinburgh, his base.

The same day Cope and his Hanoverian army landed at Dunbar, and set off for Edinburgh. Cope drew up his army in a strong position, protected by marshy ground, between Tranent and Prestonpans, to await reinforcements from Berwick-upon-Tweed. His plan appears to have been to prevent the Jacobites from advancing any further down the east coast.

The Jacobites did not wait in Edinburgh, and immediately advanced from Duddingston, on the east side of the city, towards Cope's army. On 20 September the Jacobites circled round to the south, led by a local man who knew the marches, and launched an attack from the east, taking Cope by surprise. The Hanoverian forces were almost immediately routed – in ten minutes according to some – and Cope had to flee the battle, having overslept, and rode all the

Death of Colonel Gardner, Battle of Prestonpans, engraving by R. C. Bell after Sir William Allan (Scottish United Services Museum).

way to Berwick-upon-Tweed. Much of Cope's army was caught against the estate-wall of Prestongrange House, and there died in their hundreds – 1200 were killed or wounded, and 1800 taken prisoner. There were few casualties among the Jacobites, and the Prince was lenient towards the defeated enemy, ensuring that his men took prisoners where possible.

This crushing victory was vitally important, as now virtually all Scotland was controlled by the Jacobites, with the exception of Edinburgh, Stirling and Dumbarton Castles, and the Highland forts. Cope's artillery was also seized.

The Prince returned to Edinburgh via Pinkie House, near Musselburgh to the east of the city, and for the next six weeks stayed at Holyroodhouse. His forces had grown with the arrival of the MacDonalds of Clan Ranald, as well as of Glengarry and of Glencoe, the

Stewarts of Appin, the Macphersons, the Robertsons and men from Atholl. Few recruits, only numbering some 500, joined from the Protestant south. Most of the army of 5000 were Episcopalian or Roman Catholic Highlanders or men from the north.

The Prince hoped for support from Louis XV and the French, and was persuaded to wait at Holyroodhouse.

Holyroodhouse – Bonnie Prince Charlie stayed here after the crushing defeat inflicted by his army at Prestonpans.

Small forces did arrive at Montrose and Peterhead, but not in sufficient numbers. In England a large Hanoverian army, led by General Wade, was marching north towards Scotland, and by 29 October had reached Newcastle. Disagreements between Lord George Murray, supported by other Scots, and Charles's Irish advisors worsened. Finally the Prince lost patience, and decided to march south into England, hoping for increased support.

The Jacobites set out from Edinburgh, and travelled through Pinkie, to Dalkeith House, where they stayed for two nights, then on to Thirlestane Castle, near Lauder, on 3 November. From here they arrived at Traquair House, entering through the Bear Gates. Stewart of Traquair is said to have closed the gates after the Prince left, and declared that they were not to be opened until a Stewart was once again on the throne.

They have remained closed to this day.

The army marched on southwards, and crossed the Esk into England on 8 November, having tricked Wade into thinking that they intended to invade England through Northumberland. They easily captured Carlisle Castle, which was poorly maintained and garrisoned, but were then divided about what to do next.

Wade and his army were at Hexham, and other Hanoverian armies were being raised. Some of the Highlanders began to leave the army and make their way back home. Reinforcements were needed, either from English Jacobites or from the French. Charles wanted to march to London, and eventually, after much discussion and disagreement, they set off south again.

Substantial support from England did not materialise, despite the belief there would be a general uprising.

The Jacobites proceeded down the west side of England, through Penrith, Kendall, Lancaster, Preston, Manchester and Macclesfield – only in Manchester did they find any support, some 300 new troops

Map 5: England (1715-46)

joining. Still lacking any real opposition – Murray had deceived the Hanoverians by a feint into Wales – they arrived at Derby, and here received conflicting news.

It was said that George II had packed his bags and was ready to flee the country; that the Hanoverian government was in panic; that Wales was stirring. Reinforcements had arrived at Montrose, including some large artillery pieces.

On the other hand, three separate armies were now assembled against them: General Wade at Wetherby in Yorkshire, behind them, with 8000 men; William Augustus, Duke of Cumberland and favourite son of George II, at Lichfield, north of Birmingham, with 10 000 more; and an inexperienced force at Finchley, north of London.

In Scotland there was also news that the Campbells were mustering for the Hanoverians in Argyll; Edinburgh was once again in the hands of the government; and the British navy was patrolling the seas.

A council of war was held at Derby on 6 December 'Black Friday', and although the Prince wished to advance on London, the majority opinion, led by Lord George Murray and backed by many others, was to return to Scotland. Their lines of communication were very stretched; and it was likely they would soon be surrounded by three armies. Charles wanted to go on, after all the army at Finchley should have been no match for the Jacobites, and they could have seized London. The majority opinion, however, prevailed – despite the Prince's growing anger and frustration – and the army began its well-ordered withdrawal towards Scotland.

In this Murray played a crucial role, protecting the rear of the Jacobite army on its way back to Scotland, and he even led the MacDonalds and Macphersons to victory over a small force of Hanoverian dragoons at Clifton, south of Penrith.

The Jacobites reached Carlisle on 19 December, and then returned to Scotland, recrossing the Esk and leaving a garrison of Manchester volunteers and Scots to hold Carlisle. These men quickly surrendered on the arrival of the Duke of Cumberland's army some days later, and many of their number were executed by disembowelment, while others were transported.

Drumlanrig Castle – Bonnie Prince Charlie stayed here on his way north.

The Jacobite army, meanwhile, marched north through Scotland via Nithsdale, staying at Drumlanrig Castle, Douglas Castle and then Hamilton Palace on 24 December, before approaching Glasgow, where support was decidedly lukewarm. On 26 December Charles set up his 'court' at Shawfield, but on 3 January moved to Bannockburn House, the large mansion of Sir Hugh Patterson.

Here Charles met Clementina Walkinshaw, who is said to have been a great beauty – and who became his mistress, almost immediately. Reinforcements, under Lord John Drummond, finally arrived, and the Jacobite army now numbered about 8000 men. The Jacobites besieged Stirling Castle, which was garrisoned by Hanoverian troops.

A Hanoverian force, also numbering about 8000 men, was sent north from Newcastle to relieve the castle. It was led by General Harry Hawley, who had replaced Wade. Hawley had a reputation for severity towards both his own men, strictly enforcing military discipline, as well as cruelty to the enemy. Not anticipating an encounter with the Jacobites until he reached Stirling, Hawley encamped at Callendar House, near Falkirk, on the night of 16 January 1746.

To Hawley's horror, the next morning word was brought that the Jacobites were grouping on the high ground behind the house. Hawley led his troops on a frantic scramble up the hill in the rain to meet the Jacobites; but he was too late. A fierce battle followed in the mud, and Hawley's army was routed. The fighting is said to have lasted only 20 minutes, but the victory was marred by confusion among the Jacobite army, which allowed Hawley to escape. Nevertheless, Hanoverian losses numbered some hundreds while the Jacobites lost less than 50.

But the Jacobites could not press their advantage. Hawley retreated to Linlithgow, where his troops managed to burn down the Palace, while the Jacobites returned to the ill-conceived siege of Stirling – they managed to lose some of their guns, and 30 or so men, in one exchange of fire with the castle garrison.

On the approach of Cumberland's army in early February, the Jacobites abandoned their ineffectual siege of Stirling Castle, and continued their withdrawal northwards.

Charles had wasted time and resources in an attempting to capture Stirling Castle. The Jacobites marched through Crieff, stopped at Castle Menzies for two nights, where they were entertained by the Menzies family. Cumberland's forces reached the castle four days later, threw out the family, and took over the castle.

The Jacobites marched on to Blair Atholl. Lord George attacked and damaged nearby Blair Castle, which had fallen into the hands of the Hanoverians – the last castle in Britain to be besieged.

From here the Jacobites crossed the Drumochter Pass into Strathspey, and headed for Inverness. The size of the army dwindled as men returned to their glens, many intending to rejoin to the Prince's army when the weather improved in the spring.

On the way north, Charles stopped at Moy Hall. The Campbell Earl of Loudoun, the Hanoverian commander of Inverness, learned of the Prince's whereabouts, and set out with 1500 men to capture Charles at Moy.

The situation might have been serious had not a handful of Jacobites, led by Colonel Anne (the wife of Mackintosh of Mackintosh), deceived Loudoun into thinking they were the whole of the Jacobite army. The Hanoverian force retreated in disorder, and fled back through Inverness and across the Kessock Ferry into Ross. This episode became known as the 'Rout of Moy'.

From Moy contingents of the Jacobite force were sent to capture Fort Augustus, which duly fell; others were sent to Inverurie, where Lord Lewis Gordon soundly defeated a pro-government force. The Prince himself marched on Inverness, and captured the castle, Loudoun only just escaping; and from here established himself at Culloden House, Forbes of Culloden's mansion, also visiting Kilravock Castle – followed two days later by the Duke of Cumberland – and Thunderton House in Elgin.

Cumberland's army, meantime, had advanced from Edinburgh up the east coast until it reached Aberdeen, where it halted until the weather improved. At the end of March it set out from Aberdeen to Cullen and then Elgin, and Lord Elcho, who was guarding the flank, had to retreat back to Culloden.

Inverness Castle – the present building replaced the government stronghold blown up by the Jacobites following the Battle of Culloden.

10–The Battle of Culloden 1746

The Hanoverian army, led by the Duke of Cumberland, had advanced up the east coast, where sufficient supplies could be received by sea. The Jacobites did not fare so well. Their supply arrangements broke down when John Murray of Broughton, the Prince's secretary, fell ill, much of their artillery had to be abandoned, and numbers in the force dwindled.

John Murray of Broughton, incidentally, is said to have been left to guard the Loch Arkaig Treasure, 40 000 gold coins from the French, which arrived too late to influence the outcome of the Rising. This gold was reputedly hidden. Broughton was captured, but secured his freedom by denouncing Simon Fraser, Lord Lovat. Broughton died in 1747, although it seems unlikely he would not have made some attempt to recover the gold.

Distrust had deepened between the Prince and Lord George Murray, who had finally returned to the Jacobite camp. Murray argued for disbanding into the mountains to conduct a new campaign in the spring.

But the Jacobites were still undefeated, and Charles had hopes of being reinforced from the Continent. It also seems that he had little relish for a guerrilla war in the mountains, and, besides, supplies were low. It was decided – against Murray's advice – to meet the larger, better-supplied and better-equipped Hanoverian army in an open pitched battle on Drumossie Moor, near Culloden.

As Cumberland approached from Nairn, a night attack on the Hanoverian camp was planned, as it was the Duke's birthday and the Jacobites believed they would be celebrating. But in the darkness the Jacobites lost their way and strayed into marshy ground. Eventually the Duke of Perth ordered a retreat as they could not have reached Nairn by daybreak. By the time Charles discovered the front of his army was retreating, it was too late to change the battle plan.

Arriving back at Drumossie Moor, the Jacobites were tired, hungry and dispirited – and divided: there was disagreement as to where the clans should be placed in the battle and which had precedence.

On the morning of 16 April 1746, Charles's advisors once again urged him to reconsider the wisdom of a pitched battle. But the Prince was determined to fight. To compound the misery of the Jacobites, it began to rain with a cold northeasterly wind driving into their faces. Cumberland was in no hurry, and his men rested during the morning.

Cumberland's forces consisted of about 9000 men —

Monument to the fallen at Culloden.

some 2400 cavalry and 6400 infantry – while the Jacobites numbered around half that. The battle started at about 1.00pm with the Hanoverian guns concentrating on the Jacobite artillery. When this had been suitably decimated, their pieces turned on the massed ranks of the Jacobite army. The Jacobites were drawn up on a narrow front between two walls, and many men fell.

For 20 minutes the bombardment continued, until the charge was finally ordered.

The left wing of the Jacobites, mostly MacDonalds, did not obey and held their position, while the centre veered right to avoid marshy ground and joined the right flank in a headlong charge. Many fell from the volleys of Hanoverian muskets. The Jacobites were so tightly packed that they could not use their own guns. The right and centre fell upon the Hanoverian left, and although they suffered terrible casualties, broke through. But many then fell in fire from the Hanoverian line behind.

The Hanoverian army had adopted a new method of close-quarter fighting for the battle. Rather than attacking the Jacobite head on, each Hanoverian was to stab at the man on his right; the up-raised sword arms of the Highlanders made them vulnerable to bayonet thrusts from this side. This tactic worked.

Although hopelessly outnumbered, the Highlanders fought on, until all were slain or had fallen or were thrown back.

Attempts to disengage persuaded those on the left flank, the MacDonalds, that things were going badly – and still they hesitated. MacDonald of Keppoch tried to lead his men into battle, but he was wounded and then shot down.

When Cumberland's cavalry and dragoons then swung into action, the left side retreated and the rout began. This reluctance to charge has been put down to the MacDonald's anger at not being given a more prominent position in the battle – but in truth it would have been little better than suicide to have charged.

Dragoons began pouring forward and engaged the small cavalry force protecting the Prince. Outnumbered five to one, the Jacobites fought on but suffered grievous losses. Instead of rallying his men, Charles allowed himself to be led away and fled the battlefield. As the Prince rode off, David Wemyss, Lord Elcho, (not a great fan of Charles) reportedly said: 'There goes a damned Italian coward'.

Monument to Lord Srathallan, commander of Strathallan's horse, who was slain nearby and the men of Perthshire killed in the Prince's army.

The battle was all over in an hour. Hanoverian losses were reckoned at about 350, Jacobite losses on and off the battlefield at more than 2000. It was the bloodiest of the Jacobite battles, and the last to be fought on British soil. It should be remembered, however, that more Scots fought for and supported Cumberland than Bonnie Prince Charlie.

The slaughter was not confined to the battle: it continued on until nightfall and then resumed the next morning. William Augustus, the Duke of Cumberland, well earned the name 'Butcher'. His orders were that there was to be no mercy or quarter. Jacobite wounded or prisoners were shot, bayonetted or clubbed to death.

The following day parties were sent to scour the countryside, every house and cottage in a wide area was searched for hiding wounded, who were then summarily executed, while their shelterers were also punished.

Nineteen wounded officers were taken to the wall of Culloden House, and there shot, while their skulls were bashed in with rifle buts to ensure they were dead. One man, thought to be slain, survived to tell the tale, although with a smashed jaw. Another party of 40 Jacobites were found in a thatched cottage, which was then burnt down over them.

Those among Cumberland's army, even Scots staunchly loyal to the Hanoverians such as Forbes of Culloden, who protested were themselves punished or at best ignored. All this was particularly cruel as the Jacobite army had behaved well on its travels, and had done nothing to warrant this massacre.

Worse was to follow. Martial law was imposed, with the shooting and hanging of fugitives, the driving off of stock, and the burning of houses and cottages. Prisoners captured after the battle were tried in England, because Scottish juries were thought to be too lenient. Many were executed on Tower Hill, and at Carlisle, York and at Kennington Common.

One hundred and twenty ordinary soldiers were executed, a third of them deserters from the Hanoverian army, but nearly 700 men, women and children died in jail. Two hundred were banished, and almost 1000 were sold to the American plantations. Jacobite nobles had their lands and titles forfeited, and some were executed, including

William Boyd, 4th Earl of Kilmarnock, a Colonel in the Prince's guard; the Mackenzie 3rd Earl of Cromartie; Arthur Elphinstone, 6th Lord Balmerino; and Simon Fraser, Lord Lovat. At the execution, incidentally, seating holding many of the spectators collapsed, and several were killed. Fraser is said to have remarked grimly: 'The mair mischief, the better sport'.

A massive new artillery fort was built at Fort George, although it was not completed until 1769 by when it was not needed, and new garrisons were established at Corgarff and Braemar.

The structure of the clan system was also torn down, in an attempt to destroy a very way of life forever. The authority of the clan chiefs was taken from them: by the abolition of heritable jurisdictions in 1747, which had given them the power of justice and law over their people. The Disarming Act was strictly enforced: the carrying or possession of arms was forbidden – the only implement the Highlander was allowed was a blunt eating knife. The wearing of tartan and Highland dress was banned in the Act of Proscription, with transportation for a repeated offence; even the playing of bagpipes, said to be a weapon of war, was forbidden.

When the proscription on Highland dress was lifted in 1782, few of the common people went back to wearing it – it had become the party dress of their new landlords and the garb of Highland regiments in the British army.

Fort George – this massive artillery fort was built after the Battle of Culloden.

11–The End of the Jacobites

Although Jacobite casualties at the battle had been heavy, a remnant of the army blew up the castle at Inverness, and many men went south to the barracks at Ruthven, and there gathered to await orders. Here they were joined by Cameron of Lochiel and other clan chiefs, the Duke of Perth, Lord Ogilvie, and eventually Lord George Murray. They had lost the battle, but they still had sufficient men to continue the Rising. But it was not to be. They received word from the Prince that they must do what they must to save themselves, effectively ending the Rising. The remaining Jacobites disbanded, while their leaders sought passage through the Highlands to the Continent. Murray escaped to France, and then on to exile in Germany and Holland, where he died.

When Cumberland eventually returned to London, he was given a hero's welcome and was praised by both houses of Parliament. He also received an extra £25,000 a year to his income.

Charles, meanwhile, blamed Murray for the disaster, and left his Scottish troops at Culloden. His Irish supporters were worried he would be captured, that even Scottish Jacobites might turn him in for Hanoverian gold. Charles made for Fort Augustus, and there tried to rally his men, but to no avail – although he only waited two hours. His small party reached Invergarry Castle, stronghold of the MacDonalds of Glengarry, but found it already abandoned – it was soon burnt out on the orders of Cumberland. It was decided that Charles should make for the Continent with all haste, and accompanied by only three companions he left for Arisaig, where they hoped to find a French ship.

Here they stayed for a week, but Cumberland's forces were scouring the mainland, and Charles and his companions made their way from Loch nan Uamh in a rowing boat, and headed for Eriskay in the Outer Hebrides, but a storm blew them out of their way and they landed instead on Benbecula. By then two French ships were at Loch nan Uamh, and picked up many Jacobites, including David Lord Elcho, Lord John Drummond, and the Duke of Perth. The vessels were attacked the next day by British warships, and although they managed to escape, many of the crew and passengers were killed or injured. The Duke of Perth died aboard ship. Elcho escaped to the Continent, and died in 1787.

Meanwhile the Prince had made for Stornoway on Lewis, but had been forced south again, and sheltered on South Uist. He stayed at Corodale on the island for three further weeks, and was garbed out in Highland dress; it is during this time he is said to have acquired a taste for whisky and strong drink. On the mainland, Cameron of Lochiel had been trying to raise fresh forces for the Jacobites, but Cumberland was mercilessly harrying any person suspected of having Jacobite sympathies. Troops were sent out into the Hebrides to search for Charles: the Prince's position was becoming precarious.

It was decided to smuggle Charles over to Skye, and Flora MacDonald, whose family came from the area, became involved – the Prince was to be disguised as her maid 'Betty Burke'. Flora left Charles to make arrangements, but was stopped and arrested by Hanoverian troops, only being released because her stepfather was their commanding officer. Several days later, the Prince suitably disguised in a blue and white dress, they set out for Skye and landed on Trotternish, but there were government forces everywhere. The Prince made for Portree, and then leaving Flora, crossed to the island of Raasay, but fearing discovery returned back to Skye, where he

Hills of northern Skye.

stayed until early July. He was helped by the chief of the MacKinnons, and is said to have given MacKinnon the recipe for Drambuie, a whisky liqueur (although originally made with cognac), in gratitude. The chief was later imprisoned in the Tower of London.

When her part in his escape became known, Flora MacDonald was arrested, briefly imprisoned in Dunstaffnage Castle, and sent to London. She spent a short time in the Tower and, released by the 1747 Act of Indemnity, returned to Skye where she married Allan MacDonald of Kingsburgh in 1750. Flora and her husband emigrated to America in 1774, where they fought for the Hanoverian government in the American War of Independence. She had to return to Scotland in 1779, and died on Skye.

Charles then returned to the mainland, reached Borrodale by 10 July, and made his way to Glenmoriston, where he sheltered with other fugitives for three weeks. Travelling back south, he came to Achnacarry, home of Cameron of Lochiel, but the house had also been torched by Cumberland's men. Charles joined Cameron of Lochiel on 30 August, and the men and other fugitives sheltered in 'Cluny's Cage', an ingenious hiding place made by Ewen Macpherson of Cluny from branches and thatch. Cluny had fought at Culloden, but remained a fugitive in Scotland until 1755, when he escaped to France, and died there soon afterwards.

Finally on 13 September it was reported that two French ships were at Loch nan Uamh, and the Prince hurried to the rendezvous. On 19 September he, Cameron of Lochiel and other Jacobite fugitives, boarded the two ships *Le Prince de Conti* and *L'Heureux*, and Bonnie Prince Charlie sailed away, never to return to Scotland.

Although Charles was hailed as a hero when he returned to the continent, the Jacobite cause was in its death throes, and he spent the following years roaming the countries of Europe in disguise, chasing one plot or another. In 1750 he went secretly to London to pursue his claims, and declared himself a Protestant, but it was to no avail, support had evaporated or been crushed. The Hanoverians were victorious.

In 1752 Charles asked Clementina Walkinshaw, who he had met at Bannockburn House in 1746, to join him, and they had a daughter

Charlotte the following year. Clementina, however, eventually left him as his drinking and abuse grew worse.

Charles did not visit James, his father, after returning from Scotland, and after James's death in 1766, the Pope decided not to recognise Charles as King. James VIII and III had remained a staunch Roman Catholic, and was buried in St Peter's in Rome, where the future George IV later paid for a monument, designed by Canova, to be placed over his tomb.

Charles, after several affairs (he is said to have been bisexual), married Princess Louise of Stolberg in 1772, but they had no children, meaning their was no legitimate heir to carry on the Jacobite cause. She was a girl of just 20, he a drunkard of over 50; and he is said to have beaten her. She also left him, and, as Princess of Stolberg, she was later welcomed at the court of George III.

By 1780 Charles was a lonely and abandoned figure. He invited Charlotte, his daughter by Clementina Walkinshaw, to stay with him in Rome, and made her Duchess of Albany.

Bonnie Prince Charlie, by Hugh Douglas Hamilton (SNPG).

Charles died, in the arms of his daughter, of a stroke at the age of 67 on 31 January 1788, the last rites performed by his brother Henry Benedict, Cardinal York. Charlotte, herself, was ill and died only two years later. Henry made no serious attempt to pursue the claim to the throne of either Scotland or England, and when he died in 1807, after receiving a pension from the Hanoverian government for several years, so did the Jacobite cause. Charles and Henry were buried beside their father in St Peter's in Rome.

Charlotte, the Duchess of Albany, had three illegitimate children, although two died in infancy. Her son Charles Edward, born in 1784, died as a result of a coaching accident near Dunkeld in 1854, and – although married twice – had no children.

By this time the legend of Bonnie Prince Charlie and the Jacobites had almost totally obscured the ruin the cause had left in its wake. Bad luck had played its part in this failure, of course, but poor leadership, lack of resources, the Stewart's adherence to the Roman Catholic faith, and shifting European politics had also played their part. In the end, however, it was a simple lack of support from both England and the south of Scotland which doomed the Risings.

The final irony is, perhaps, that shortly after the collapse of the 1745-46 Rising thousands of Highlanders – many from what were Jacobite clans – were recruited into the Hanoverian army, where they played an often vital, and valiant, part in the fighting which strengthened and expanded the British Empire.

It had further appeal for the British government, as William Pitt, the British Prime Minister, put it: not many of them would return.

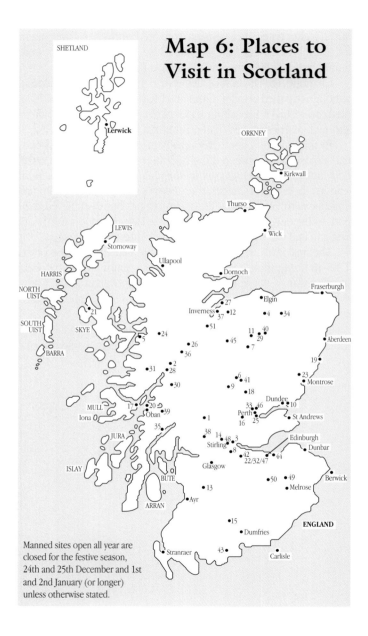

Map 6: Places to
Visit in Scotland

SHETLAND

Lerwick

ORKNEY

Kirkwall

Thurso

Wick

LEWIS

Stornoway

Ullapool

Dornoch

HARRIS

NORTH
UIST

Fraserburgh

27
Elgin

• 12
Inverness • 4 • 34
37

SOUTH
UIST

SKYE

• 21

• 5 • 24

• 51

11 40
• 29
45 7

Aberdeen

• 26
36

19

BARRA

• 31 • 2
28

• 6 • 41
9

• 23
Montrose

• 30

• 18

Dundee

33 46 • 10
MULL 17 • 20 • Perth
Iona 16 25 St Andrews
Oban 39

• 1

38
14
48 3
Stirling 8

Edinburgh
Dunbar

JURA

35

42
22/32/47 44

Glasgow

50 • 49
Berwick
13 Melrose

ISLAY

BUTE

Ayr

ARRAN

• 15

ENGLAND

Dumfries

43

Stranraer

Carlisle

Manned sites open all year are
closed for the festive season,
24th and 25th December and 1st
and 2nd January (or longer)
unless otherwise stated.

Places to Visit

P   Parking
S   Sales Area
R   Refreshments
WC   Toilet
£   Admission Charge
HS   Historic Environment Scotland
       (historicenvironment.scot)
NTS   National Trust for Scotland
       (www.nts.org.uk)

1 Achallader Castle

Off A82, 3.5 miles NE of Bridge of Orchy.
NN 322442 50
Not much remains of a 16th-century tower house. It was burnt in 1603 by the MacGregors, and in 1689 by Jacobites. The castle was the scene of a conference in 1691 between the Campbell 1st Earl of Breadalbane and Jacobite Highland chiefs, who agreed to an armistice.

2 Achnacarry

Off B8005, 9 miles NE of Fort William.
NN 175878 41 PH34 4EJ
Site of 17th-century house of the Camerons of Lochiel, the ruins of which remain, destroyed by Hanoverian troops after the Rising of 1745. The Camerons were forfeited, although they recovered the property in 1784. A converted cottage houses the **Clan Cameron Museum**. Disabled access/WC.
Tel: 01397 712090
www.clancameronmuseum.co.uk
Museum open April to October.

   P   S   WC   £

3 Alloa Tower

Off A907, in Alloa, Clackmannan.
NTS NS 889925 58 FK10 1PL
Alloa Tower is an impressive altered 15th-century keep, although it may incorporate older work. The top floor has a fine and rare medieval timber roof.

The property was given to Sir Robert Erskine, Great Chamberlain of Scotland, in 1360, and has remained with his descendants, the Earls of Mar. Mary, Queen of Scots, visited. 'Bobbing John', 6th Earl of Mar, lived here and was leader of the Jacobites in the 1715 Rising. Collection of portraits of the Erskine family. Disabled WC and access to ground floor only.
Tel: 01259 211701
Open April to October, Friday to Monday; also May to Aug, open Thurs.

   P Nearby   S   WC   £

4 Balvenie Castle

Off A941, N of town of Dufftown, Moray.
HS NJ 326409 28 AB55 4GH
In a pleasant location, Balvenie Castle consists of a large ruinous courtyard castle, with a 13th-century curtain wall and surrounding ditch. It was seized by the Jacobites in 1689, but in 1715 was held against them. It was abandoned in 1718, although a Hanoverian force briefly held it in 1746. Disabled WC.
Tel: 01340 820121
Open daily April to September.

   P   S   WC   £

5 Bernera Barracks

Off A87 at Shiel Bridge, 0.3 miles N of
Glenelg, Highlands.
Ruin or site NG 815197 33
Built to control the crossing to Skye, Bernera
Barracks, dating from the 1720s, consists of
impressive ruined ranges of buildings around
a courtyard, and had accommodation for over
200 men. The garrison was reduced after the
failure of the Rising in 1746, and abandoned
about 1800. The road to Glenelg mostly
follows the course of an old military way.
View from exterior.

6 Blair Castle

Off A9, 1 mile NW of Blair Atholl,
Perthshire.
NN 867662 43 PH18 5TL
Blair Castle, a rambling white-washed
castellated mansion of the Dukes of Atholl,
incorporates the 13th-century Comyn's
Tower. The castle was garrisoned by Bonnie
Dundee, John Claverhouse, in 1689, and it
was here that his body was brought after
Killiecrankie, to be buried in the nearby
graveyard at St Brides. The Earls of Atholl
were made Marquises, then Dukes in 1703.
  Bonnie Prince Charlie stayed here in 1745.
In 1746 the castle was held by Hanoverian
forces, and attacked and damaged by Lord
George Murray, brother of the Duke of Atholl.
It is the last castle in Britain to have been
besieged. Collections of paintings, arms,
armour, china, costumes and Jacobite
mementoes. Garden. Disabled facilities.
Tel: 01796 481207
www.blair-castle.co.uk
**Open daily April to October: may be
open in winter, tel to confirm.**

P S R WC £

7 Braemar Castle

On A93, 0.5 miles NE of Braemar,
Kincardine & Deeside.
NO 156924 43 AB35 5XR
Braemar Castle is an altered 17th-century
L-plan tower house, surrounded by 18th-
century artillery defences. In 1689 the

Erskines held the castle for William and Mary,
but after the death of the Earl of Mar, it was
captured and torched by Jacobites under
Farquharson of Inverey. However, 'Bobbing
John', 6th Earl of Mar, led the 1715 Rising.
  The castle passed to the Farquharsons, but
in 1748 was leased by the government, and
between 1748 and 1797 was used as a
barracks, some of the walls bearing the graffiti
of the garrison. The Farquharsons reoccupied
the castle in the early 19th century, and it is
now run by the local community on a fifty-
year lease. Many interesting rooms.
Tel: 01339 741219
www.braemarcastle.co.uk
Open Apr-Oct, Wed-Sun; Jul-Aug, daily.

P S WC £

8 Callendar House

Off A803, in Falkirk.
NS 898794 65 FK1 1YR
Callendar House, a large ornate mansion with
towers and turrets, incorporates a 15th-
century castle of the Livingstone Earls of
Callendar. The Livingstones were forfeited for
their part in the 1715 Rising, and the house
was leased to the Boyd Earl of Kilmarnock,
although he was beheaded for his part in the
1745 Rising. Bonnie Prince Charlie stayed
here in 1745; and General Hawley and a
Hanoverian army camped here before going
on to defeat at the nearby Battle of Falkirk in

1746. The building has a restored kitchen of the 1820s. Disabled access; lift. Park.

www.falkirkcommunitytrust.org
Tel: 01324 503772
Open all year: Wed-Sun

P Nearby S R WC £

9 Castle Menzies

Off B846, 1.5 miles NW of Aberfeldy, Perthshire.

NN 837496 52 PH15 2JD

Castle Menzies is a fine altered and extended 16th-century Z-plan tower house, a property of the Menzies family. The castle was captured and occupied by Jacobites in 1715. Bonnie Prince Charlie stayed here for two nights in 1746, but four days later the family were thrown out and the castle was taken by Hanoverian forces, led by the Duke of Cumberland. Interesting museum about the Menzies clan. Disabled access to tea room; gift shop; part of ground floor.

Tel: 01887 820982
www.castlemenzies.org
Open April or Easter to October daily, Sun PM only.

P S R WC £

10 Claypotts Castle

Off A92, 3.5 miles E of Dundee.

HS NO 452319 54

An unusual and impressive building, Claypotts is a Z-plan tower house, consisting of a main block and two large round towers at opposite corners. It was a property of John Graham of Claverhouse, Viscount Dundee.

Tel: 01241 878756 in advance for
internal access or view exterior.

11 Corgarff Castle

Off A939, 10 miles NW of Ballater, Aberdeenshire.

HS NJ 255086 37 AB36 8YP

Corgarff Castle consists of a much-altered 16th-century tower house, with 18th-century pavilions and star-shaped outworks. The Erskine Earls of Mar acquired the lands in 1626. The castle was burnt by Jacobites in 1689 to deny its use to the Government, and again in 1716 by Hanoverians to punish John 6th Earl of Mar. The Jacobites occupied it during the Rising of 1745 when it was torched again, and in 1748 the government bought Corgarff and turned it into a barracks. Short walk to castle. Exhibition: one of the floors

Corgarff Castle

houses a restored barrack room. There is a fine stretch of the old military way nearby.

Tel: 01975 651460

Open April to September, daily

`P S £`

12 Culloden

On B9006, 5 miles E of Inverness, Highland.
NTS NH 745450 27 IV2 5EU

It was here on the bleak moor of Drumossie that on 16 April 1746 the Jacobite army of Bonnie Prince Charlie was crushed by Hanoverian forces led by the Duke of Cumberland – the last major battle to be fought on British soil. The Jacobites were tired and hungry, and the Hanoverians had a better equipped and larger army: the battle turned into a rout and many Jacobites were slaughtered after the battle. Sites of interest include Old Leanach Cottage, Graves of the Clans, Well of the Dead, Memorial Cairn, Cumberland Stone and Field of the English. The new visitor centre houses a Jacobite exhibition and historical display, and there is an interesting audiovisual programme. Disabled access to visitor centre and WC.

Tel: 01463 796090

www.nts.org.uk/Culloden/Home/

Site open all year; visitor centre all year except 24-26 Dec & 31 Dec-2 Jan

`P S R WC £`

13 Dean Castle

Off B7038, 1 mile NE of Kilmarnock, Ayrshire.
NS 437394 70 KA3 1XB

Interesting and well preserved, Dean Castle consists of a 14th-century keep and 15th-century palace block within a courtyard enclosed by a curtain wall. The castle was held by the Boyd Earls of Kilmarnock.

The 4th Earl was Privy Councillor to Bonnie Prince Charlie during the Rising of 1745. He was a Colonel in the Prince's guard, but was captured in 1746 after the Battle of Culloden, and executed by beheading. His lands were forfeited, but the 5th Earl recovered the estates in 1748. This was apparently predicted when sometime before the Rising servants were terrified by an apparition of Boyd's severed head rolling about the floor.

The castle now houses a museum, containing a collection of armour and musical

Culloden Moor – monument.

instruments, and is surrounded by a public park. Disabled access to some of the castle.

Tel: 01563 554743
www.eastayrshireleisure.com
Open all year: castle currently closed due to maintenance

`P S R WC £`

14 Doune Castle

Off A820, SE of Doune, Stirlingshire.
His Scot NN 728011 57 FK16 6EA
Standing on a strong site in a lovely location, Doune Castle, built in the 14th century, consists of two strong towers linked by a lower range within a courtyard. The castle was held by Government troops during the Risings of 1689 and 1715. It was taken by Jacobites in 1745, and used as a prison, although many of the prisoners escaped. Exhibition.

Tel: 01786 841742
Open daily all year.

`P S WC £`

15 Drumlanrig Castle

Off A76, 3 miles NW of Thornhill, Dumfriesshire.
NX 851992 78 DG3 4AQ
Drumlanrig Castle is a large castellated mansion, with ranges of buildings around a courtyard, and higher rectangular towers at the corners. It was built between 1675 and 1689 by the architect William Wallace for William Douglas, 3rd Earl of Queensberry, who was made Duke in 1684. Bonnie Prince Charlie stayed here in 1746. The castle passed to the Scott Dukes of Buccleuch in 1810. Fine collection of pictures, as well as many other works of art. Jacobite mementoes. Gardens. Visitor centre. Disabled access.

Tel: 01848 331555
www.drumlanrig.com
Open some days Apr & May, then Jul-Aug, daily; grounds, Apr-Sep.

`P S R WC £`

16 Drummond Castle

Off A822, 2.5 miles SW of Crieff, Perthshire.
NN 844181 58 PH7 4HN
Built on a rocky outcrop, Drummond Castle consists of a 15th-century keep and later extensions, and it was held by the Drummond Earls of Perth. The castle was slighted after having been occupied by Hanoverian troops during the Rising of 1715. The 5th Earl had commanded the Jacobite cavalry at the Battle of Sheriffmuir that year, and the 6th Earl commanded the left side of the Jacobite army at the Battle of Culloden in 1746. The family was forfeited, although the Earldom of Perth was later recovered. The castle and magnificent formal garden featured in the film version of *Rob Roy*. Partial disabled access.

Tel: 01764 681433
www.drummondcastlegardens.co.uk
Castle not open. Gardens open Easter and then daily May to October.

`P S WC £`

17 Duart Castle

Off A849, 3 miles S of Craignure, Mull.
NM 749354 49 PA64 6AP
An extremely impressive and daunting fortress, Duart Castle consists of a large 13th-century curtain wall, enclosing a courtyard with a keep on the outside of the wall. The castle was built by the MacLeans of Duart,

who remained staunch supporters of the Jacobites throughout the Risings. Although garrisoned, the castle was not used as a residence, but troops were stationed here after 1746. Duart houses a display of clan memorabilia. Tea room and shop located in converted byre.

Tel: 01680 812309
www.duartcastle.com
Castle open April to mid October, daily

P S R WC £

18 Dunkeld

Off A923, Dunkeld, Perthshire.
NO 013424 53

Dunkeld was besieged by the Jacobites in 1689 after the Battle of Killiecrankie. The Cameronian garrison managed to hold the town, within the Cathedral precinct, although most of it was burnt. The cathedral is a fine building dating from the 13th century, the choir of which is used as a parish church, while the nave is ruined.

P Nearby

19 Dunnottar Castle

Off A92, 2 miles S of Stonehaven, Kincardine & Deeside.
NO 882839 45 AB39 2TL

Built on an excellent defensive site on a high promontory 160 feet above the sea, Dunnottar Castle is a spectacular ruined courtyard castle. It was a property of the Keith Earls Marischal.

In 1685 Covenanters, numbering some 167 women and men, were packed into one of the cellars during a hot summer and 9 died while 25 escaped.

The castle was held for William and Mary in 1689, and many Jacobites were imprisoned here. The Earl Marischal threw in his lot with the Jacobites during the Rising of 1715, and was subsequently forfeited. The Duke of Argyll partly destroyed Dunnottar in 1716, and it was more fully slighted in 1718.

Getting to the castle involves a walk, steep climb, and a steeper one back.

Tel: 01569 766230
www.dunnottarcastle.co.uk
Open daily all year (weather permitting).

P S WC £

20 Dunstaffnage Castle

Off A85, 3.5 miles NE of Oban, Argyll.
HS NM 882344 49 PA37 1PZ

On a promontory in the Firth of Lorn, Dunstaffnage Castle consists of a massive 13th-century curtain wall, with round towers, and an altered 16th-century gatehouse. It was held by the Campbell Earls of Argyll, and the

9th Earl torched the castle in 1685. Government troops occupied the castle during the Risings of 1715 and 1745, and Flora MacDonald was briefly imprisoned here after helping Bonnie Prince Charlie. Disabled WC.

Tel: 01631 562465
Open all year daily except closed Thu and Fri October to March.

P S WC £

21 Dunvegan Castle

Off A850, 1 mile N of the village of Dunvegan, Skye.
NG 247491 23 IV55 8WF

Continuously occupied by chiefs of MacLeod since 1270, Dunvegan Castle is a large mansion which incorporates an old castle. There are many mementoes of Bonnie Prince Charlie and Flora MacDonald. Other interesting items include the Fairy Flag, and

Rory Mor's Horn. Garden. Boat trips. Disabled WC.

Tel: 01470 521206
www.dunvegancastle.com
Open daily April to mid October.

`P S R WC £`

22 Edinburgh Castle

Off A1, in the centre of Edinburgh.
HS NT 252735 66 EH1 2NG

Standing on a high rock, Edinburgh Castle was one of the strongest and most important fortresses in Scotland. The Jacobites failed to take it in both the 1715 and 1745 Risings, although some of them were later imprisoned here. Many of the existing fortifications and buildings date from the 17th and 18th centuries.

The castle is the home of the Scottish Crown Jewels, and the Stone of Destiny – on which the Kings of Scots were inaugurated – and is an interesting complex of buildings with spectacular views over the capital. Visitors with a disability can be taken to the top of the castle by a courtesy vehicle; ramps and lift access to Crown Jewels and Stone of Destiny. Disabled WC and some access.

Tel: 0131 225 9846
www.edinburghcastle.scot
Open all year.

`P Nearby S R WC £`

23 Edzell Castle

Off B966, 6 miles N of Brechin, Angus.
HS NO 585693 44 DD9 7UE

Edzell Castle consists of an early 16th-century tower house with ruinous ranges of buildings around a courtyard. A large pleasance, or garden, was created in 1604, and surrounded by an ornamental wall, the fine carved decoration of which is unique. It was a property of the Lindsay Earls of Crawford, but they had to sell the property in 1715, because of huge debts, and it was bought by the Maule Earl of Panmure. The Maules were forfeited for their part in the 1745 Rising, and the castle was garrisoned by Hanoverian troops, who did much damage. Exhibition. Garden. Disabled WC and access.

Tel: 01356 648631
Open daily April to September.

`P S WC £`

24 Eilean Donan Castle

On A87, 8 miles E of Kyle of Lochalsh, Highland.
NG 881259 33 IV40 8DX

One of the most beautifully situated of all Scottish castles, Eilean Donan consists of a 13th-century wall surrounding a courtyard with a strong 14th-century keep. It was a property of the Mackenzie Earls of Seaforth, William 5th Earl, had it garrisoned with Spanish troops during the Rising of 1719, but

Edinburgh Castle.

three frigates battered it into submission, and it was blown up from within. The ghost of one of the Spanish troops, killed either at the castle or the Battle of Glenshiel, is said to haunt the castle. Visitor centre to open in summer 1998. Exhibitions. Disabled WC.

The battle of Glenshiel took place at the head of Loch Duich, near Shiel Bridge, and the site is marked by an information board.

Tel: 01599 555202
www.eileandonancastle.com
Open daily February to December

P	S	R	WC	£

25 Elcho Castle

Off A912, 4 miles E of Perth.
HS NO 165211 58 PH2 8QQ
Impressive and well preserved, both stronghold and comfortable residence, Elcho Castle is a 16th-century Z-plan tower house. The Wemyss family held the property from 1468, and were made Lords Elcho in 1633. David, Lord Elcho, fought and survived the Battle of Culloden on the Jacobite side in 1746, but had to flee to France.

Tel: 01738 639 998
Open daily April to September.

P	S	WC	£

26 Fort Augustus

Off A82, at Fort Augustus, Highland.
NH 380095 34
Part of the barracks survives behind the Lovat Arms Hotel, while more remains survive within the abbey buildings. The barracks, built in 1716, were subsequently strengthened and enlarged by General Wade, and named Fort Augustus. The fort was captured by the Jacobites in 1746, but restored and occupied until the 1850s. It was sold to Lord Lovat in 1857, and presented by him to the Benedictine Order in 1876, although this has since closed. In the village is the **Clansmen Centre** with a museum, croft house and displays of weaponry (01320 366444; www.clansmencentre.uk).

27 Fort George

Off B9006, 11 miles NE of Inverness, Highland.
HS NH 763566 27 IV2 7TD
Fort George is an outstanding example of a Georgian artillery fort. It was built after the Rising of 1745-46 to designs of William Skinner, and was completed in 1769, by which time it was not needed. It extends over 16 acres and could accommodate nearly 2000 men. Reconstruction of barrack rooms in different periods, and display of muskets and pikes. Disabled access and WC.

Tel: 01667 460232
Open daily all year.

P	S	R	WC	£

28 Fort William

Off A82, 1.5 miles NE of Fort William, Highland.
NN 120754 41
The village of Fort William is named after the now ruinous fort, which was built by General Monck for Cromwell during the 1650s, then reconstructed and renamed in 1690, during the reign of William of Orange. It was bombarded in the spring of 1746 by Jacobites, but could not be taken. It was garrisoned until 1866, after which most of it was demolished. The West Highland Museum has information about the fort.

View from exterior.

P Nearby

29 Glenbuchat Castle

Off A97, 4.5 miles W of Kildrummy, Aberdeenshire.
HS NJ 397149 37 AB36 8TN
Glenbuchat Castle is a roofless 16th-century Z-plan tower house. Brigadier-General John Gordon of Glenbuchat fought for the Jacobites in the 1715 and 1745 Risings, and led the Gordons and Farquharsons at the Battle of Culloden in 1746 – when already 70. He was hunted after the battle, but managed to escape to Norway, disguised as a beggar, and died in France.

View from exterior.

P

30 Glencoe

On A82, 17 miles S of Fort William, Highland.
NTS NN 127564 41 PH49 4HX

Glencoe, one of the most picturesque areas of Scotland, was the site of the infamous massacre of 1692, executed by government forces under Campbell of Glenlyon. Thirty-eight members of the MacDonalds of Glencoe, including their chief MacIain, were slaughtered by men from the garrison of Fort William, who had been billeted on the MacDonalds.

One of the sites of the massacre at Inverigan can be visited; as can the Signal Rock, reputedly from where the signal was given to begin the massacre.

The visitor centre has a video programme on the massacre, as well as an exhibition on the history of mountaineering. Walks. Climbing. Disabled access to ground floor; WC.

Tel: 01855 811307
Site open all year; visitor centre open daily all year, except closed around Xmas and New Year

P S R WC £

31 Glenfinnan

On A830, 18.5 miles W of Fort William, Highland.
NTS NM 906805 41 PH37 4LT

It was here that on 19 August 1745 the standard was raised by the Jacobites under Bonnie Prince Charlie for James VIII and III, so beginning the 1745 Rising. The Glenfinnan Monument, set in a picturesque location, was built in 1815 to commemorate the many who fought and died for Bonnie Prince Charlie. Visitor centre features an audio programme about the campaign, and other displays. Disabled access to exhibition, snack bar and shop; WC.

Tel: 01397 722250
Monument accessible all year; visitor centre open all year.

P S R WC £

32 Holyroodhouse

Off A1, Edinburgh.
NT 269739 66 EH8 8DX

Holyroodhouse consists of ranges surrounding a rectangular courtyard, one of which dates from the 16th century. The present building was designed by Sir William Bruce for Charles II in 1671-8. Bonnie Prince Charlie stayed here in 1745 for six weeks, and

Glenfinnan.

79

held court after the Battle of Prestonpans; while the Duke of Cumberland made it his residence after Culloden. The palace is the official residence of the monarch in Scotland. Collections of portraits, including the Prince.

www.royalcollection.org.uk
Tel: 0131 556 5100   Open daily all year except when monarch is in residence and 25-26 December.

`P Nearby  S  R  WC  £`

33 Huntingtower Castle

Off A85, 3 miles NW of Perth.
HS NO 083252 58 PH1 3JL

A well-preserved and interesting building, Huntingtower consists of a 15th-century keep, a 16th-century L-plan tower house, and a later connecting range. There are fine painted ceilings, mural paintings and plasterwork, as well as decorative beams in the hall.

The property was held by the Ruthvens from the 12th century, and was originally called Ruthven Castle. In 1600 the family were forfeited after the 'Gowrie Conspiracy', and their name proscribed. The castle, renamed Huntingtower, later passed to the Murray Dukes of Atholl. Lord George Murray, Bonnie Prince Charlie's general in the 1745 Rising, was born here.

Tel: 01738 627231
Open daily all year except closed Thursdays and Fridays October to March.

`P  S  WC  £`

34 Huntly Castle

Off A920, N of Huntly, Aberdeenshire.
HS NJ 532407 29 AB54 4SH

A fine building with a long and violent history, Huntly Castle consists of a strong ruinous 15th-century keep in a courtyard with the remains of outbuildings. It was a property of the Gordon Earls of Huntly, and was garrisoned by Hanoverian soldiers, during the Rising of 1745-6, but by then had been abandoned as a residence. Exhibition.

Disabled WC.
Tel: 01466 793191
Open daily all year except closed Thursdays and Fridays November to March.

`P  S  WC  £`

35 Inveraray Castle

Off A83, N of Inveraray, Argyll.
NN 096093 56 PA32 8XE

The seat of the Campbell Dukes of Argyll. The present castle was begun in 1743, and is a symmetrical classical mansion with towers and turrets, which was remodelled by William and John Adam. The castle houses many interesting rooms, with collections of tapestries and paintings, and superb displays of weapons. Rob Roy MacGregor's sporran and dirk handle are on display. The Clan Room features information of special interest to members of Clan Campbell. Disabled access to ground floor only,

www.inveraray-castle.com
Tel: 01499 302203
Open April to October, daily

`P  S  R  WC  £`

36 Invergarry Castle

Off A82, 7 miles SW of Fort Augustus, Invergarry, Highland.
NH 315006 34 PH35 4HW

An impressive ruin, Invergarry Castle is a large 17th-century L-plan tower house. It was built by the MacDonalds, or Clan Ranald, of Glengarry. In 1688 Alasdair MacDonald of Glengarry fortified the castle for James VII, but eventually submitted to the government of William and Mary in 1692. It was retaken by Alasdair Dubh of Glengarry in 1715, but recaptured by Hanoverian forces a year later. The castle was back in the hands of the MacDonalds by 1731, and during the Rising of 1745-6 was twice visited by Bonnie Prince Charlie. It was burnt by Hanoverian forces after the Rising, and left a ruin.

Ruins can be seen from grounds of Glengarry Castle Hotel (01809 501254; www.glengarry.net) – the castle is in a dangerous condition and should not be entered.

P Nearby

37 Inverness Castle
Off A82, in Inverness, Highland.
NH 667451 26 IV2 3EG
Site of the royal castle of Inverness, which was much modified in the 18th century. It was captured by the Jacobites in 1715, but was retaken by Hanoverian forces the same year. It was repaired in 1718, but was finally captured and blown up by the Jacobites in 1746 after the Battle of Culloden. A mock castle of 1835 was built on the site – only the well from the old castle surviving.

38 Inversnaid Barracks
Off B829, Garrison, 16 miles NW of Aberfoyle, Stirlingshire.
NN 348097 56
Little remains of a barracks, dating from 1719. The barracks were built after the Rising of 1715 to protect against the MacGregors, and Rob Roy's men attacked the workmen during construction. The barracks were commanded by General Wolfe, before he was a general, but were abandoned by 1800. In 1820 part of the building was used as an inn, but it had been demolished by 1828.

39 Kilchurn Castle
Off A85, 2 miles W of Dalmally, Argyll.
HS NN 133276 50 PA33 1AF
A picturesque and much photographed ruin, Kilchurn is a courtyard castle of the 15th century, much extended with late 17th-century barrack-blocks. It was built by the Campbells of Glenorchy, later Earls of Breadalbane, and was occupied until 1740 when they moved to Taymouth. Kilchurn was garrisoned by Hanoverian troops in 1745. The castle can be reached on foot from the A85 under the nearby railway viaduct. Caution is advised as the route can flood.
Open daily April to September.

P Nearby

40 Kildrummy Castle
Off A97, 10 miles SW of Alford, Aberdeenshire.
HS NJ 454164 37 AB33 8RA
Although now ruinous, Kildrummy Castle, built in the 13th century, was one of the largest and most powerful early castles in Scotland. The castle was badly damaged in 1690, when it was burned by Jacobites, but was complete enough for the John, 6th Earl of Mar, to use it as his base when he led the Rising in 1715. After the collapse of the Rising, Kildrummy was deliberately dismantled and used as a quarry. Disabled WC.
Tel: 01975 571331]
Open daily April to September.

P S WC £

41 Killiecrankie
On B8079, 3 miles N of Pitlochry, Perthshire.
NTS NN 917627 43 PH16 5LG
Set in a fine and picturesque wooded gorge, it was near here that in 1689 that the Jacobites, led by John Graham of Claverhouse, Viscount Dundee, defeated a government army. Claverhouse was mortally wounded at the battle, and the Jacobites disbanded after failing to capture Dunkeld. At Killiecrankie is the 'Soldier's Leap', where

Killiecrankie

one government soldier escaped from Jacobite forces by jumping across the River Garry. Exhibition in the visitor centre features the battle, with models and maps. Disabled WC.

Tel: 01796 473233
Site open all year; Visitor Centre open daily Easter or April to October.

P S R WC £

42 Linlithgow Palace

Off A803, in Linlithgow, West Lothian.
HS NT 003774 65 EH49 7AL
A magnificent ruin, Linlithgow Palace consists of ranges of buildings set around a rectangular courtyard, and may include 12th-century work. There is a fine carved fountain in the courtyard, which operates on Sundays in July and August. James VII, when Duke of York, stayed here, as did Anne, Bonnie Prince Charlie in 1745, and the Duke of Cumberland. In 1746 General Hawley retreated here after being defeated by the Jacobites at the nearby Battle of Falkirk. His soldiers started fires to dry themselves, and

the palace was accidentally set blaze. It was never restored. Partial disabled access.
Tel: 01506 842896
Open all year.

P S WC £

43 Orchardton Tower

Off A711, 4 miles S of Dalbeattie, Galloway.
HS NX 817551 84 DG7 1QH
Orchardton is a round ruinous tower house. It was a property of the Cairns, but passed to the Maxwells. During the Rising of 1745, one of the family, Sir Robert Maxwell, was wounded and captured at Culloden in 1746 and taken to Carlisle for trial and probable execution. He tried to destroy his personal papers, but was prevented, and his commission as an officer in the French army discovered. He was subsequently treated as a prisoner of war, and was sent to France rather than being executed. He later returned to Orchardton.
Open April to September.

P

Places to Visit

44 Prestonpans

Off A198, E of Prestonpans, East Lothian.
NT 403744 66
The site of the Jacobite victory in 1745, led by Bonnie Prince Charlie, over a government army under Sir John Cope. Cope fled all the way to Berwick-upon-Tweed.

A plain stone cairn with the date 1745 stands near the site (by the B1316). There is also a viewpoint with a timeline, a waymarked trail, and an audiovisual display in the doocot of **Bankton House** telling the story of Colonel Gardiner, who was slain at the battle. The government baggage train was captured at nearby **Cockenzie House**, which is open to the public most days and has a cafe and fine gardens.

Site open all year.

45 Ruthven Barracks

Off A9, 1 mile S of Kingussie, Highland.
HS NN 764997 35 PH21 1NR
Built on the earthworks of an old castle, ruined ranges of buildings surround a courtyard. In 1718 the castle here was demolished and replaced by the barracks for Hanoverian troops. Ruthven was held by government forces in 1746, but was eventually taken and burnt by Jacobite forces and they gathered here following defeat at Culloden in 1746 but soon disbanded.

Open all year.

P

46 Scone Palace

Off A93, N of Perth.
NO 114267 58 PH2 6BD
Scone Palace, a fine castellated mansion, dates from 1802, but incorporates part of the palace built by the Ruthvens in the 1580s. Scone passed to the Murrays, who were made Earls of Mansfield in 1776. Scone was the site of the inauguration of Scottish kings and Charles II was crowned here.

James VIII and III held 'court' here in 1716, and Bonnie Prince Charlie visited in 1745.

Collections of furniture, clocks, needlework and porcelain. Gardens. Disabled facilities and WC.

Tel: 01738 552300
scone-palace.co.uk
Open daily April to October.

P S R WC £

47 Scottish National Portrait Gallery

Off A1, Queen Street, Edinburgh.
NT 255743 66 EH2 1JD
Among the many portraits of notable Scots, including Kings and Queens, the gallery also has pictures of many Jacobites, including James VII, James VIII, and Bonnie Prince Charlie. Disabled facilities and WC.

Tel: 0131 556 8921 / www.national galleries.org/portraitgallery
Open all year.

P Nearby S R WC

48 Stirling Castle

Off A872, in Stirling.
HS NS 790940 57 FK8 1EJ
Standing on a high rock, Stirling Castle consists of a large courtyard castle, which dates from the 12th century. The outer defences were constructed in Jacobite times, and much of the medieval castle was also altered for artillery. The garrison harried the Jacobites during both the 1715 and 1745 Risings, and the Jacobites besieged the castle after the Battle of Falkirk in 1746, although not very successfully. After 1745, the castle was subdivided for use as a barracks. In 1964 the army left, and much of the castle has been or is being restored. Exhibition, introductory display, medieval kitchen display. Disabled access and WC. Ticket includes admission to Argyll's Lodging.

Tel: 01786 450000
www.stirlingcastle.scot
Open all year except 25-26 December.

P S R WC £

49 Thirlestane Castle

Off A68, NE of Lauder, Borders.
NT 534479 73 TD2 6RU

Thirlestane Castle is a 16th-century castle, which was considerably enlarged in the 1670s and later. It was home to John Maitland, Duke of Lauderdale, a very powerful man in Scotland in the 17th century, whose ghost is said to haunt the castle. Bonnie Prince Charlie stayed here in 1745. Good collection of portraits, as well as furniture and china. Exhibition of historical toys and Border country life. Disabled access to tea room.

Tel: 01578 722430
www.thirlestanecastle.co.uk
Open approx May to September:
check days and times with castle.

P S R WC £

50 Traquair House

Off B709, 1 mile S of Innerleithen, Borders.
NT 330354 73 EH44 6PW

Reputedly one of the oldest continuously inhabited houses in Scotland, Traquair is an altered and extended tower house, which may incorporate work from the 12th century. Bonnie Prince Charlie stayed here in 1745, entering through the now famous Bear Gates. One story is that the 5th Earl closed and locked them after Charlie's departure, swearing they would not be unlocked until a Stewart once more sat on the throne of the country. They are still locked. The house has a collection of Stewart mementoes. Working 18th-century brewery. Gardens and maze. Craft workshops. Gift and Cashmere shop. Disabled WC and limited access to house.

Tel: 01896 830323
www.traquair.co.uk
Open daily April to October; also
open Saturday and Sunday in
November.

P S R WC £

51 Urquhart Castle

Off A82, 1.5 miles E of Drumnadrochit, Highland.
HS NH 531286 26 IV63 6XJ

Standing on the shore of Loch Ness, Urquhart Castle consists of a ruinous 13th-century castle of enclosure with a curtain wall, gatehouse, and later tower house. The castle held out against the Jacobites in 1689, but was dismantled in 1691 to prevent them using it, and the gatehouse blown up with gunpowder. New visitor centre. There have been many sightings of the Loch Ness Monster from near the castle – and there are two monster exhibition centres in nearby Drumnadrochit.

Tel: 01456 450551
Open all year – walk to castle.

P S R WC £

Some Other Places of Interest

Stranraer Castle [01776 705544] (Castle of St John), which is open to the public, was used by John Graham of Claverhouse, later Viscount Dundee, while suppressing Covenanters in Galloway. A memorial to the **Wigtown Martyrs** stands in the graveyard at Wigtown. There are many other Covenanter memorials. **Argyll's Lodging** [01786 450000], Stirling, was the townhouse of Archibald Campbell, 9th Earl of Argyll, who was executed in 1685. It is in the care of Historic Scotland and open to the public.

Cawdor Castle [01667 404401; www.cawdorcastle.com] is open to the public and the grounds of **Dalkeith House** [0131 654 1666; www.dalkeithcountrypark.com]; while **Culloden House** (01463 790461; www.cullodenhouse.co.uk) is a hotel and **Thunderton House** was a public house, although this is closed at time of writing. Bonnie Prince Charlie stayed at all four.

Other properties which are open to the

public with Jacobite connections include **Castle Fraser** [NTS; 01330 833463], **Castle Stalker** [01631 740315; www.castle stalker.com], **Delgatie Castle** [01888 563479; www.delgatiecastle.com], and **Drum Castle** [NTS; 01330 700334]. A cairn at **Loch nan Uamh** marks the place where Bonnie Prince Charlie left Scotland. James VIII, Bonnie Prince Charlie and Henry Benedict, Cardinal York, are buried in **St Peter's** in the Vatican in Rome. A monument, designed by Canova and paid for by the Hanoverian King George IV, marks their tomb.

Blackness [HS; 01506 834807] and **Dumbarton** [01389 732167] Castles were both garrisoned against the Jacobites and are open to the public, being in the care of Historic Scotland. Many miles of **military ways** survive throughout Scotland, linking the various garrisons and forts, mostly built by General George Wade and Major William Caulfield. Particularly good stretches can be found on the West Highland way, between Glasgow and Fort William, while many modern routes follow the course of military ways. Two fine bridges are also worth a mention. The **Tay Bridge**, which crosses the river just north of Aberfeldy, was built in 1733 to designs of William Adam. **Invercauld Bridge**, to the north of Braemar, was built in 1753 over the River Dee.

Carlisle Castle [EH; 01228 591922], which was captured and held by the Jacobites in 1745, is in the care of English Heritage and open to the public. **Berwick Barracks** [EH; 01289 304493], standing in the walled town, was built between 1717 and 1741, and is also in the care of English Heritage.

Some Useful Websites

Historic Environment Scotland
historicenvironment.scot
National Trust for Scotland
www.nts.org.uk
English Heritage
www.english-heritage.org.uk

Most manned sites open all year are closed for the festive season, 24th and 25th December and 1st and 2nd January (or longer).

Blackness Castle

Map 7: *Outlander* locations
www.thecastlesofscotland.co.uk/the-best-castles/outlander/

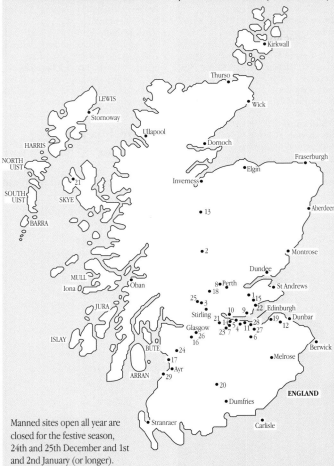

Kirkwall

Thurso

Wick

LEWIS

Stornoway

Ullapool

Dornoch

HARRIS

Fraserburgh

NORTH UIST

Elgin

Inverness

SOUTH UIST

SKYE

21

Aberdeen

BARRA

• 13

• 2

Montrose

MULL

Oban

Dundee

Iona

8 • Perth

18

St Andrews

JURA

25 •

3

• 15

Stirling

10 9

22

Edinburgh

21

28

19

Dunbar

Glasgow

13 5

11 27

12

23 7 4

6

26

16

ISLAY

BUTE

• 24

Melrose

17

ARRAN

Ayr

29

Berwick

• 20

ENGLAND

Manned sites open all year are
closed for the festive season,
24th and 25th December and 1st
and 2nd January (or longer).

Dumfries

Stranraer

Carlisle

Historic Environment Scotland (HES)
historicenvironment.scot
National Trust for Scotland (NTS)
www.nts.org.uk

Outlander

Locations in Scotland from the popular TV series, produced by Sony Pictures Television and based on the books by Diana Gabaldon, with the backdrop of the Jacobite Risings from 1743.

1 Falkland (Inverness)

On A912, 4 miles N of Glenrothes, Fife. Pretty village with the magnificent royal palace. Inverness in the 1940s and the exterior of Mrs Baird's B&B is the Covenanter Hotel (covenanterfalkland.co.uk, 01337 857163) (Season 1). The village was then used as Inverness in the 1960s (Season 2).

2 Kinloch Rannoch (Criagh na Dun)

Off B846, 3.5 miles E of village of Kinloch Rannoch, in Tay Forest Park, Tullochroisk farm, Perthshire.
NN 710571 42 PH16 5QF
Picturesque and remote part of Scotland, although there are no stones at site. The iconic stone circle that transports Claire to 1743 in the first episode, and is in further episodes (Season 1 & 2, and Season 4).
On private land: access is possible but not during lambing or other agricultural activity.

3 Doune Castle (Castle Leoch)

Off A820, SE of Doune, Stirlingshire.
HES NN 728011 57 FK16 6EA
Large and impressive old fortress in a lovely spot. Features as Castle Leoch, home of the Mackenzies in the 18th century and visited by Claire, the exterior, courtyard and great hall being used, although the kitchen and other rooms, such as Claire's chamber, were a set (Season 1). Claire's herb garden was filmed at Culross Palace. Also see entry for Doune Castle on page 75.
Tel: 01786 841742
Open daily all year.

P S WC £

4 Midhope Castle (Lallybroch/Broch Tuarach)

Off A904, 1 mile W of Hopetoun House, Abercorn, West Lothian.
NT 073787 66 EH49 7NB
Atmospheric old tower house on the Hopetoun estate. Broch Tuarach or Lallybroch, home of Jamie Fraser, having been left to him by his parents, and his sister Jenny and her husband, and visited by Claire after they are wed (Seasons 1-3).
hopetoun.co.uk/estate/outlander-at-hopetoun
0131 331 2451
Castle accessible Apr-Dec (check website for closures during the period): tickets must be bought in advance from Hopetoun House ticket kiosk or Hopetoun Farm Shop: view from exterior only.

P nearby £

Doune Castle (Castle Leoch)

Midhope Castle (Lallybroch)

5 Blackness Castle (Fort William)

Off B903 or B9109, 4 miles east of Bo'ness, West Lothian.
HES   PH34 4EJ
Large and grim old stronghold. The castle is used as Fort William, headquarters of Black Jack Randall, and Jamie is flogged in the courtyard (Season 1 & 2).
Tel: 01506 834807
Open all year, closed Thu & Fri in winter.

P S WC £

6 Glencorse Old Kirk

Off A701 or A702, 2 miles N of Penicuik, Midlothian. *EH26 0NZ*
Atmospheric old church, on private ground, used as a wedding venue. Jamie and Claire are married here (Season 1).
www.glencorsehouse.com
Wedding venue.   Tel: 01968 676406

7 Linlithgow Palace (Wentworth Prison)

Off A803, in Linlithgow, West Lothian.
HES   NT 003774   65   EH49 7AL
Magnificent ruin of a royal palace. The entrance and corridors were used as Wentworth Prison, where Jamie is abused by Black Jack (Season 1). Also see entry on page 82.
Tel: 01506 842896
Open all year.

P S WC £

8 Tibbermore Church (Cranesmuir Church)

Off A85, 3 miles E of Perth, Perthshire.
NO 052234   58   PH1 1QJ
Fine old abandoned church, dating from the 17th century, in an interesting burial ground. The church was used for the notorious witch trial, when Geillis and Claire are accused (Season 1).
srct.org.uk   Tel: 0131 563 5135
Access to the church can be arranged.

9 Aberdour Castle

Off A921, Aberdour, Fife.
HES   NT 183854   66   KY3 0SL
Large, partly ruinous castle with fine gardens. Jamie is healed here after being rescued from Black Jack, the old kitchen and long gallery being used for filming (Season 1).
Tel: 01383 860519
Open all year; closed Thu & Fri in winter.

P R S WC £

10 Culross (Cranesmuir)

On A912, 4 miles N of Glenrothes, Fife.
KY12 8JH
Picturesque and largely unaltered village, dating from the 17th and 18th centuries. The village of Cranesmuir and location of Claire's herb garden (Culross Palace, NTS). Also used for the Jacobite encampment and hospital scenes (Season 2).
Tel: 01383 880359 (NTS)
Village access at all times; Culross Palace (NTS), open Apr-Oct, daily.

11 Hopetoun House

Off M90, South Queensferry, Edinburgh.
EH30 9RW (for satnav)
Large and impressive mansion house in fine grounds. Home of the Duke of Sandringham and rear steps used for a sword fight, while grounds scene of the duel between the Duke and leader of the MacDonalds (Season 1). Courtyard behind tearoom features as a street in Paris (Season 2). Hopetoun is also a location in Season 3 & 4.
www.hopetoun.co.uk/estate/
outlander-at-hopetoun
0131 331 2451
House open Easter-late Sep.

P R S WC £

12 Preston Mill

Off B1377, E of East Linton, East Lothian.
NTS EH40 3DS
Scenic water mill with pond and nearby doocot. Jamie takes a dip in the pond, as well as other scenes (Season 1). **01620 860426**
Open Easter, then May-Sep, Thu-Mon.

13 Highland Folk Museum

Off A9, Newtonmore, Highland. *PH20 1AY*
Excellent museum. Scenes include when Dougal collects the rent (Season 1).
highlifehighland.com   01540 673551
Open Apr-Oct, daily.

14 Bo'ness and Kinneil Railway

Off M9, Bo'ness, West Lothian. *EH51 9AQ*
Heritage railway with steam of diesel trains. Wartime London railway station where Claire and Frank part (Season 1).
bkrailway.co.uk   01506 822298
Check website for timetable.

15 Balgonie Castle (Eldridge Manor)

Off A911, 3 miles E of Glenrothes, Fife.
NO 313007 58 KY7 6HG
Interesting and impressive old castle. Eldridge Manor, home of the MacRannochs, Claire devises the plan to free Jamie using Highland cattle (Season 1).
balgoniecastle.co.uk
Open from April, Wed-Sun.

16 Pollok Country Park

Off M77, Pollok, S of Glasgow. *G43 1AT*
Fine wooded park and gardens, the former grounds of Pollok House (NTS). Used as the grounds around Castle Leoch (Season 1), then as countryside between Le Havre and Paris (Season 2). **www.glasgow.gov.uk**
Country park open all year.

17 Troon

Off A78, Troon, Ayrshire.
Pleasant seaside town on Firth of Clyde. The harbour is where Claire, Jamie and Murtagh board a ship to France (Season 1).

18 Drummond Castle Gardens (Versailles)

Off A822, 3 miles S of Crieff, Perthshire.
NN 844181 58 PH7 4HN
Beautiful formal gardens of the historic castle. Used as the gardens and orchard of the Palace of Versailles (Season 2).
drummondcastlegardens.co.uk
Tel: 01764 681433
Gardens open Easter, then May-Oct; castle not open.

P S WC £

19 Gosford House (Versailles stables)

Off A198, 2 miles NE of Longniddry, East Lothian. *EH32 0PX*
Impressive grand mansion in extensive parkland. Used as Versailles (Season 2) and Helwater and Ellesmere Manor (Season 3).
gosfordhouse.co.uk   01875 870808
Open Easter, then some Thu-Mon in Jul & Aug.

P £

20 Drumlanrig Castle (Bellhurst Manor)

Off A76, 3 miles N of Thornhill, Dumfries and Galloway. *DG3 4AQ*
Impressive old mansion in extensive parkland. Used as Bellhurst Manor, outside and inside (Season 2). Also see page 75.

drumlanrigcastle.co.uk 01848 331555
Open May-Aug.

P R S WC £

21 Callendar House

Off A803, E of Falkirk, West Lothian.
NS 898794 65 FK1 1YR
Large gothic mansion in wooded country
park. The old kitchen was used for Bellhurst
Manor (Season 2).
www.falkirkcommunitytrust.org
Tel: 01324 503772 Open all year.

P R S WC

22 Dysart harbour (Le Havre)

Off A955, E of Kirkcaldy, Fife. *KY1 2TQ*
Picturesque old harbour in historic village.
Used as Le Havre, where Jamie and Claire
land in France, and the St Germains
warehouse (Season 2). The two-masted
lugger, seen in the harbour, is berthed in
Anstruther harbour in the East Neuk village.
Access at all times.

23 Muiravonside Country Park

Off B825, 4 miles W of Linlithgow. *EH48 6LW*
Country park with woods, parkland and
gardens. Location of the Battle of
Prestonpans, the government camp and
English countryside (Season 2).
www.falkirkcommunitytrust.org
Tel: 01324 590900 Open all year.

24 Dean Castle (Beaufort Castle)

Off B7038, 1 mile NE of Kilmarnock. *KA3 1XB*
Impressive old castle (closed for renovation)
in wooded park. Used as Beaufort Castle,
home to Lord Lovat (Season 2).
eastayrshireleisure.com 01563 554734
Country park open all year.

25 Deanston Distillery

Off A84, 1.5 miles SW of Doune. *FK16 6AG*
Distillery in a former cotton mill in pretty
spot. In Le Havre, Jamie's cousin's wine
warehouse (Season 2).
deanstonmalt.com 01786 843010
Distillery tours all year.

26 Glasgow

Off M8, Glasgow.
George Square in the centre of Glasgow
(G2 1DU) was the location of Frank's
proposal to Claire in the 1940s (Season 1).
Glasgow Cathedral (HES; open all year,
except Sun am; 0141 552 6891/0988,
G4 0QZ): Imposing gothic cathedral. The
crypt was used as L'Hopital de Anges in Paris,
where Claire works (Season 2). **Glasgow
University** (gla.ac.uk, 2 miles W of George
Square, G12 8QQ) was used as Harvard,
where Frank taught, while nearby
Kelvingrove Park (www.glasgow.gov.uk,
open all year, G3 6BQ) is the location of
Boston Park (Season 3).

27 Craigmillar Castle (Ardsmuir Prison)

Off A7 or A6095, SE of Edinburgh. *EH16 4SY*
Large ruinous castle. Used as Ardsmuir
Prison, where Jamie is imprisoned (Season 3).
Tel: 0131 661 4445
Open all year, closed Thu & Fri in winter.

P S WC £

28 Edinburgh

Off A1, Old Town, Edinburgh.
The Signet Library has a stunning interior
(Colonnades Cafe, near St Giles Cathedral:
thesignetlibrary.co.uk, 0131 226 1054,
EH1 1RF). Used as the Governor's Mansion
in Jamaica. **Bakehouse Close**, one of the
best preserved of the capital's narrow old
streets, off Royal Mile (Canongate, EH8 8PA).
Location of Jamie's print shop, where he and
Claire are reunited after their separation.
Tweeddale Court, another atmospheric old
close, off the Royal Mile (High Street,
EH1 1TE). Scene of the market when Claire
is reunited with Fergus (Season 3).

29 Dunure

Off A719, 8 miles SW of Ayr.
Pretty seaside village on Firth of Clyde. The
harbour is where Claire and Jamie leave
Scotland in search of Young Ian. Dunure
Castle is Silkie Island. (Season 3).